Strategy from

SELF-DEVELOPMENT FOR MANAGERS

A major series of workbooks for managers edited by Jane Cranwell-Ward.

This series presents a selection of books in workbook format, on a range of key management issues and skills. The books are designed to provide practising managers with the basis for self-development across a wide range of industries and occupations.

Each book relates to other books in the series to provide a coherent new approach to self-development for managers. Closely based on the latest management training initiatives, the books are designed to complement management development programmes, in-house company training, and the management qualification programmes such as CMS, DMS, MBA and professional qualification programmes.

Other books in the series:

Thriving on Stress
(Second Edition)
Jane Cranwell-Ward

Managing Change
Colin Carnall

Effective Problem Solving
Dave Francis

**Step by Step Competitive
Strategy** (Second Edition)
Dave Francis

**Improving Environmental
Performance**
Suzanne Pollack

The New Flexi-manager
David Birchall

Negotiating a Better Deal
P. Fleming

**Managing International
Business**
Neil Coade

Time Management
Chris Croft

Accounting for Managers
Roger Oldcorn

Developing Assertiveness
Anni Townend

The Self-reliant Manager
Chris Bones

Effective Marketing
Geoffrey Randall

**Developing the Manager as a
Helper**
John Hayes

Making Sense of the Economy
Roger Martin-Fagg

Jane Cranwell-Ward is at Henley Management College. She is the author of *Managing Stress* (Pan, 1986).

Strategy from the Inside Out

Dominic Swords
Director of Studies
Henley Management College

Ian Turner
Director of Studies
Henley Management College

Australia · Canada · Mexico · Singapore · Spain · United Kingdom · United States

THOMSON LEARNING ™

Strategy from the Inside Out

Copyright ©1997 Dominic Swords and Ian Turner

First published by International Thomson Business Press

Press is a division of Thomson Learning
The Thomson Learning logo is a trademark used herein under license.

British Library Cataloguing-in-Publication Data
A catalogue record for this book is available from the British Library

First edition 1997

Reprinted 2000 by Thomson Learning
Typeset by J&L Composition Ltd, Filey, North Yorkshire
Printed in the UK by Clays Ltd, St Ives plc
Printed in the Croatia by Zrinski d.d.

ISBN 1–86152–192–8

Thomson Learning
Berkshire House
168–173 High Holborn
London WCIV 7AA
UK
http://www.thomsonlearning.co.uk

——Contents

Figures and tables   vi
Series editor's preface   vii
Preface   ix
Introduction   1

 1 The need for strategic thinking   4
 2 The search for competitive advantage   15
 3 Key success factors: what drives business logic
    and how are these drivers changing?   26
 4 Strategies for medium-sized companies:
    lessons from research   38
 5 Understanding the economy   47
 6 Analysing the business environment   53
 7 Understanding the competitive dynamics
    in your industry   68
 8 Pulling it all together   81
 9 Creating the right strategy   89
10 Enacting strategy   116

    Appendix A: Sources of industry data   126
    References   128
    Further reading   130
    Index   131

Figures and tables

FIGURES

1.1 Planning styles profile I   7
1.2 Planning styles grid   9
1.3 Planning styles profile II   10
1.4 Missions and objectives   14
3.1 The life cycle   28
3.2 Economies of scale   31
3.3 The experience curve   32
5.1 GDP forecasts 1997   51
6.1 Turbulence scale   55
7.1 Porter's five forces model   73
7.2 Strategic group analysis diagram   77
9.1 Strategic alternatives   91
10.1 Reconciliation qualities for performance and future growth   118

TABLES

1.1 A mission to succeed   12
6.1 Managing environmental uncertainty   57
6.2 Environmental analysis   63
6.3 World tyre industry 1995 – 2000   65
9.1 Criteria for evaluating strategic options   106
9.2 Strategies for industry stages   108
9.3 Strategic option criteria matrix   111

Series editor's preface

Strategic capability is no longer confined to a small group of people operating in a strategic planning department of a large company or to directors of small to medium-sized businesses. Today, a broad cross section of managers need to be able to contribute to strategic thinking within their organizations.

Managers need to have a framework for structuring their strategic thinking. By undertaking a strategic review, managers can contribute to the competitive positioning of their organizations and help ensure appropriate strategic decisions are taken.

Strategy from the Inside Out has been written in a practical way and will help managers think logically as they undertake a strategic analysis of their own organization. The process is well supported by practical examples of well known organizations to help managers increase their understanding of the frameworks being used.

A workbook format has been followed, regular exercises helping the reader apply the strategic process to his or her own organization. Those managers who complete the exercises will develop greater insight of competitive strategy within their own business sector. *Strategy from the Inside Out* is primarily written for managers employed in small to medium-sized businesses, but managers in large organizations contributing to strategy formulation within their business area will also benefit from reading this book.

Ian Turner and Dominic Swords are both full-time strategy faculty members at Henley Management College. Apart from teaching strategy, Ian is programme director of Distance Learning MBA programmes. Dominic has responsibility for Corporate Qualification programmes. They both actively seek new and innovative ways of teaching strategy, Dominic is involved with the Centre for Innovation at Henley.

Strategy from the Inside Out is the latest title in the Self Development for Managers Series. The series aims to help managers develop skills and capabilities needed to successfully develop their management careers. The series develops strategic capability, personal skills including time management, assertiveness and negotiating. It also helps managers develop functional capability such as marketing and finance.

Jane Cranwell-Ward
Series Editor

Preface

This book represents the outcome of several years of collaboration in developing and applying strategic concepts together at Henley Management College. During that time, we have as teachers, sought ways to demonstrate and explain the application of strategic concepts, in the management development programmes which we have run together at Henley. At the same time, we have also been involved individually, and jointly, with several organizations which have been grappling with the task of developing their own competitive strategy. Through this interplay of our academic work, and responding to the demands of companies trying to develop robust strategies with limited time and resources, we have been able to develop and refine our approach. This approach, we hope, should enable strategic concepts – some very simple, and some more arcane – to be employed within any organization.

In the course of our work, we also became aware of a gap in the market for a book aimed primarily at medium-sized companies. Here we should acknowledge the debt that we owe to Professor Bernard Taylor at Henley whose path-breaking work on high growth medium-sized companies we have drawn on heavily here. We would also like to thank the various organizations with which we have worked over the years, which have provided us with the raw material for a lot of the illustrations in this book. Our MBA students at Henley, many of them successful executives and entrepreneurs in their own right, have also contributed to the development of our ideas and the enlargement of our knowledge base.

In the preparation of this book, we have had the invaluable counsel of the editorial staff at International Thomson Business Press, whilst the enthusiasm of the series editor Jane Cranwell-Ward has encouraged us to see the project through to completion.

Finally we would like to thank April Burt, Kiki Foster and Carol Lockhart for their contribution in producing the typescript.

Dominic Swords and Ian Turner

Introduction

WHAT THIS BOOK IS ABOUT

This is a book about strategic thinking in organizations. Unlike some other conventional books on strategy our starting point is the organisation itself and its distinctive capabilities. The book is designed for a practitioner audience – people in business who are preoccupied with where their organizations are going and how they are going to successfully compete in the market place. The book is informed by some of the latest research on strategy in real organizations and includes examples drawn from companies large and small both in the UK and abroad. It is not, however, an academic text and the aim of the book is to produce, as an output, a set of decisions on a company's strategy which will have been arrived at through a methodical and systematic process driven by the different chapters in this book.

WHO THE BOOK IS FOR

The prime target group for this book is managers in what we would term small to medium-term enterprises, manufacturing or services, or executives in charge of divisions or business units within larger corporations. It can be used to benefit by directors and chief executives of such companies as well as by individuals who may be charged to drive a strategy creating process, either from within a strategic planning function, or from the business development, marketing or finance roles. This book is not, primarily, aimed at large multi-divisional, multinational corporations. It is also not primarily focused on the needs of very small businesses, particularly those that are in the start-up phase, although both of these categories of business could read this book to advantage.

WHY THIS BOOK HAS BEEN WRITTEN

This book has been written to fill.a need that our own teaching and consultancy experience has revealed for a concise practical text which deals with the problems faced by a whole swathe of organizations out in the real world whose needs and strategic preoccupations are not fully reflected in standard academic strategy texts. Thus the type of questions we will address, the illustrations and the exercises are tailored for this specific category of company.

HOW TO USE THIS BOOK

The structure of this book is based upon a specific logic which is designed to accompany a sequential process of strategic thinking and decision making within organizations. As the title suggests, we start by focusing in on the organisation itself. In Chapters 1 and 2 we look at the sources of competitive advantage, trying to identify what it is that the company does which is distinctive and cannot easily be replicated by competitors. In Chapters 3 and 4 we turn to look at the key success factors for competing within industries and in particular how small and medium-sized companies survive and grow. In Chapters 5 to 7 we broaden the focus by analysing the company's business environment. This is to allow the company to develop a view of what prospects are likely to emerge over the coming years within its environment and what threats need to be addressed. These chapters also look at the pattern of competition and the structure of industries and offer insights on how this can affect the attractiveness of industries and the sort of strategies which are likely to be successful. In Chapters 8 to 10 we move from analysis to decision and action. By this point the company should be in a position to take the critical decisions about its future direction.

The format of the book allows preliminary decisions to be taken on a reflective basis at the end of each of the chapters and to be recorded in suitable pro forma sheets. Chapter 8 in particular provides an overview of how these pro formas can be combined and how they in turn flow into the ultimate decision making and strategic action list. Finally, we recognize that no book of this length can hope to be exhaustive. In many ways we will probably raise more questions in your mind than we would answer. This is inevitable and to be welcomed. In Appendix A and the Further Reading section you will find a number of sources – books, journals and some data services – which you can turn to if you are looking for further information on particular topics.

1 *The Need for Strategic Thinking*

INTRODUCTION

Managers in small and medium-sized companies often instinctively dismiss strategy. They see it as being inappropriate to their situation. Often they equate strategy to planning. Planning is seen as a bureaucratic, paper-driven process, acceptable, and even necessary, in large organizations where large sums of money are involved in major decisions like the acquisition of a company or the launch of a new product. Even in businesses that are conventionally well run, with strong controls over short term financial expenditure and income, it is often argued that they have neither the resources nor the management time, nor even the need to engage in strategic planning.

Let's try to address some fallacies here.

Strategy equates to planning

Corporate planning was a process introduced in to many large organizations, both in the public and private sectors since the 1960s. It originated principally in the United States. The idea underpinning formal strategic planning was that strategic decisions were different qualitatively from administrative and operational decisions taken in organizations, in the sense that they needed to take account of future developments, and issues that were external to and outside the control of the organization. For this reason, it was believed that unless there was a formal mechanism for taking such decisions organizational inertia would always prevail.

In fact, as we now know, organizational inertia in a lot of large companies proved too difficult even for formal corporate planning to overcome: the processes themselves were often criticized as being bureaucratic and time consuming and the outcomes in terms of strategic change were often perceived to be deficient. For these reasons in recent years even in many large organizations the strategic planning process has been severely streamlined and largely devolved to responsible managers at each level within the organization.

Most large organizations still have a planning process, even though it may have been simplified and speeded up. The complexity of the business and the long term pay back points for capital investments means that they need a framework within which they can work dictating a concerted approach towards strategy.

But strategy, of course, is not the same as planning. Strategy, in the sense of exploring new directions for an organization to move into, goes on independently of any formal planning process, even in large organizations: discussions at mealtimes, around coffee machines, to and from work often revolve around issues to do with strategy and are important in terms of exploring alternative options, gathering information and testing the robustness of existing strategies in an ever-changing world. You *don't* have to introduce a formal annual strategic planning system culminating in the production of a five-year corporate plan with voluminous appendices issued as an edict from the board via the corporate planning system and cascaded down the organization only to lie unopened in the drawers of the middle managers who are tasked with implementing it. You *do* have to take the opportunity periodically, particularly when a major change occurs within the businesses environment, to reassess where the business is going and consider its ability to compete within the market place.

Large companies need strategic planning because they are dealing with the deployment of large scale resources

Of course, it is true that in the aircraft manufacturing industry or the nuclear power industry where projects are large and payback periods extended, companies will tend to adopt more formalized approaches to strategic planning. But even in smaller organizations the nature of some of the decisions taken in capital expenditure, marketing or recruitment in relation to their total size may be just as significant. Decisions like: Should we open another branch? Do we need a broader portfolio? Do we need a more active approach to exporting? These are just as important strategically to an organization in that stage of its development. Of course we have to be realistic. Most companies are not strategically driven at the outset. Given the odds against survival in business start-ups, perhaps this is just as well! In the early stages of development, the style of leadership and management in a company is often entrepreneurial and short term in its focus: paying bills, generating cash flow and establishing the product or service in the market place takes overriding precedence. Generally the need for strategy in an organization is triggered by a particular event or a culmination of a series of events which causes an organization to reassess its approach: the prospect of a listing on the stock market, for instance, or the arrival of a new CEO. The fact that you are reading this book, indeed, indicates that you have probably reached that point in the organization's development. Maybe you feel that the organization has been successful in its early stages, has grown quickly and has established itself in the market place, but that things are proceeding in too *ad hoc* a fashion. You see that resources are not deployed in their most effective manner, opportunities are being missed, people are too busy to raise their heads above the grind of everyday operations. If so, then the chances are that it is time the company engaged in some strategic thinking.

STRATEGY STYLES AND APPROACHES

You can still think strategically without having to buy in to the full panoply of corporate planning. Indeed, we would argue that the approach to strategy that you take will vary according to the type of organization that you are. Figure 1.1 shows in diagrammatic form the three main dimensions along which approaches to strategy can vary.

1   In some organizations strategy is the preserve of the people or person at the top of the organization. They set the general direction and issue plans or instructions to those beneath them about how they should be deployed in practice. This is a traditional 'top-down' approach to planning and contrasts with, at the other extreme, a style where the organization encourages actively the participation of the employees at different levels who, on the assumption that they each possess vital elements necessary to

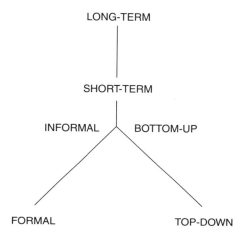

Figure 1.1   Planning styles profile I

constructing a strategy, are encouraged to contribute to the formulation of the company strategy. These are the extremes. In between, of course, one often finds organizations that have combinations of this. For example, the centre will lay out the general corporate direction, and then invite proposals from operating units within the general framework of the strategy.

2   Some businesses operate a highly formalized process of planning which is often an extension of the budgeting and/or the capital expenditure process. In such organizations there is an annual rhythm to the planning process with set dates for the submission and agreement of strategic plans. Again, this is often part of, or in addition to, the budgeting process. At the other end of the extreme are organizations where strategy is an informal and infrequent procedure which may be prompted by an important change in the company, for example the decision to float on the stock market, or just a general feeling of unease in top management that something should be done.

3   The third dimension is the planning horizon. Some organizations spend a lot of time gazing into the future even to the extent, as we shall see, of engaging in quite rigorous economic forecasting. An aircraft manufacturer, for example, will produce annually a set of

forecasts for aircraft demand over a twenty-year period. Of course such manufacturers recognize the impossibility of achieving precision over such a long period. But they are often dealing in huge lumps of capital investment. For example, the development of a new aeroplane may cost several hundreds of millions of pounds. The pay back period may be a decade or more and the plane may ultimately be in service for over twenty years. For these reasons these companies feel they need to analyse future demand. At the other end of the spectrum, of course, many companies, particularly smaller ones in fragmented industries who have little market control, operate on the basis of very short-term planning horizons. A lot of firms in service industries are like this. Such companies rarely have formal plans of longer than a year for example, and in some cases their planning horizon is a matter of months. In between these extremes many manufacturing companies claim to be operating on five-year strategic plans, although in reality often the first year is the budget and only the subsequent two years after that are considered in any depth.

Exercise 1   Plot your approach to strategy

Use the grid in Figure 1.2 to plot your own company's approach to strategy along these three dimensions. Use the comment column to justify your conclusions and to give any reasons why the approach has been taken. When you have done that turn to the diagram in Figure 1.3, transfer your assessment from Figure 1.2 on to the diagram to produce a planning styles profile or shape.

Some of the key drivers in the choice of planning styles are the following:

- The degree of environmental uncertainty or instability – typically stable environments will encourage longer term, more formal approaches to strategy, whilst more turbulent conditions will encourage more short term and *ad hoc* approaches
- Ownership – certain forms of ownership seem to encourage particular approaches to strategy, for example, in family businesses approaches to strategy are often top-down and informal emanating from the family or from the proprietor. In state owned businesses or public sector organizations, strategy is often formal and top-down, driven very much by the need to show public accountability.

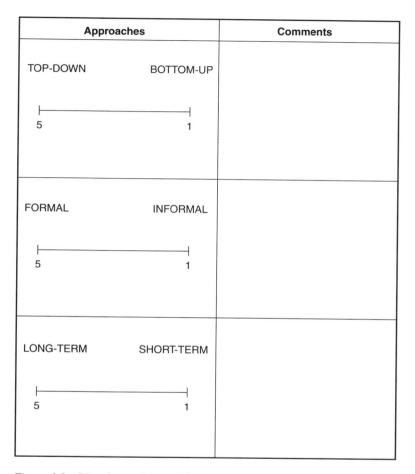

Figure 1.2 Planning styles – grid

- Capital intensity – industries which require large lumps of capital investment, for example in new projects, plant and equipment or acquisitions, often require a more long term and more formal approach to strategy.
- Industry culture – some industries encourage a particular approach to strategy. For example the construction industry is renowned for a down-to-earth action-oriented approach to management which is averse to reflection or planning.

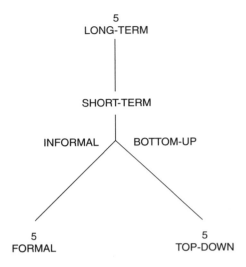

Figure 1.3   Planning styles profile II

- National cultures – some cultures are more predisposed towards planning than others. It is often said for example that the British genius is for 'muddling through' rather than for planning and this contrasts with, for example, a more methodical, formalized approach in German companies. Japanese companies can often be very long term in their approach but also surprisingly informal.
- Competitive dynamics – fragmented markets, such as office supplies where many small players compete for business, often encourage a short-term sales driven approach to business strategy.

GETTING THE 'MOST' OUT OF STRATEGY

Strategy can clearly operate at a number of different levels within organizations and conceptually it is often useful to distinguish between levels in a hierarchy. This hierarchy is often referred to as MOST.

- Missions
- Objectives
- Strategy
- Tactics.

Missions

Mission statements are often derided within organizations as being vacuous wordy documents principally designed for public consumption rather than as a basis for action. This is a shame, because the definition of a mission can be a useful starting point for a business. When defining a mission statement try to make it as short and as memorable as possible and avoid insipid feel-good phrases like 'we are a people company'. There are three main components to a mission statement – purpose, vision or direction, and values.

Purpose

What business are we in? This is the fundamental starting point for all strategy. The definition of the scope of the business, 'what's in' and, just as important, 'what's out' is critical. Are we a provider of office equipment, for example, or do we focus on document reproduction? Some companies try to avoid foreclosing on alternatives at this stage. Rentokil, for example, has a broad and flexible scope but a very specific objective: its 'consistent aim is to provide for its shareholders a growth of at least 20% per annum in profits and earning per share.' It may be worthwhile revisiting the mission statement later on in the light of your analysis of the company's situation.

Vision or direction

Essentially you should address the question: Where does this company see itself in the next three to five years? (Or whatever your timescale is.)

Values

Some companies from the outset try to incorporate a philosophy of business within their mission statement, for example, Body Shop or Ben and Jerry's Ice-cream, both firms which have clearly defined sets of values. If you articulate cherished principles, be prepared to be held to them!

Have a look at some examples of mission statements from well-known companies in Table 1.1. Notice how they embody in their different ways elements of these components.

Objectives

Objectives should naturally flow from the definition of the mission statement. Corporate objectives can be expressed in a number of

Table 1.1 A Mission to Succeed (*Source*: Company Reports)	
Company	*Statement of missions or business scope*
Christian Salvesen	'The company is focused on providing business to business services which have three key attributes, namely, they are essential and critical to the customer's business, and they are complex either in managerial or technological terms'
Medeva	'The goal is to build a significant and self-sustaining pharmaceutical company which is not dependent on its own primary research for new products.'
Unitech	'The company is a worldwide manufacturer of electronic components and controls. The three core businesses are power supplies, component and control products.'
Compass Group	'The mission is to be "a leading world food service organization with strong market positions in the UK, Continental Europe and the USA, together with small developing businesses in Eastern Europe, South America and Asia . . . through the determined pursuit of three guiding principles: providing the best quality food and service to suit each location and working in the closest cooperation with clients and customers.'

different ways. You may wish to set commercial objectives and they in turn may be couched in terms of market share, sales growth, return on investment, shareholder value etc. Objectives should be sufficiently specific that they are capable of being measured subsequently against targets and the time horizon for their achievement should be specified. Ideally, objectives should be ambitious enough to stretch the organization into excelling itself, without demoralizing employees too much with the prospect of the gap that they still have to close. Other, non-commercial, objectives are also common: for example quality, safety or environmental awareness. Corporate objectives can only really be defined in relation to the company's stakeholders. These are the organizations or individuals who can affect whether a firm attains its long-term objectives. They may be:

- shareholders
- major customers
- suppliers
- partners
- key employees
- financial institutions
- non-governmental organizations
- government bodies, etc.

Exercise 2

Review this list and identify for yourself who the prime stakeholders are in your organization.

Strategy

There is no universal agreement on what constitutes a strategy. Most aspects of operational management can at some time or other assume strategic importance to the survival of an organization. There is however broader agreement on what sort of decisions have to be made. These include the following.

- What direction should the company grow – should it 'stick to its knitting' and try to expand its share of its existing market or should it broaden its product range or its geographical scope or diversify into a completely new area?
- What position should it adopt along the value chain – should it try to integrate backwards towards the source of supply or forwards towards its buyers? Or should it try to isolate one particular part of the value chain in which it has a competitive advantage?
- How should the company seek to compete in terms of its marketing positioning and its underlying core competences?
- How should these strategies be pursued – organically, through some kind of merger or acquisition or through collaborative activity?

Tactics

Strategy of course was originally a military term, and in the military they distinguish between strategy, which is about how you conduct a campaign and tactics which is about how you fight the battle. In business terms tactics can be said to be anything within the operations of a company which translates the overall strategy into sets of actions.

Often this means breaking down the 'grand strategy' into discrete chunks for particular parts of the organization, departments, divisions or units. Increasingly, it means applying project management techniques – the use of milestones, the establishment of a 'critical path' – to the implementation of strategy.

Exercise 3

Figure 1.4 shows where you will find a number of questions relating to your company's mission and objectives. If you already have a set of missions or objectives then you need to review these at this point. If not then it is a good idea to spend some time with the management team going through these questions.

Our mission is:

(*Enter here*)

The mission statement:

- expresses the purpose of the organization (*Y/N*)
- defines the scope of the business (*Y/N*)
- indicates where the organization is intending to be in the future (*Y/N*)
- Includes any principles or values which the organization holds dear (*Y/N*)

Our objectives are:

(*Enter here*)

These objectives are:

- specific (*Y/N*)
- measurable (*Y/N*)
- achievable (*Y/N*)
- realistic (*Y/N*)
- timebound (*Y/N*)
- acceptable to our stakeholders (*Y/N*)
- consistent with our mission (*Y/N*)

Figure 1.4   Missions and objectives – how do they measure up?

2   *The Search for Competitive Advantage*

Have you ever wondered how some companies manage to survive? Some companies seem to be adept at struggling on, often for decades and over several generations, with no apparent strategy. Equally, there are others which go under when times are tough, the recession bites, or competition hots up.

Even established companies which have sustained a competitive edge over several years can find themselves wrong-footed by the rapid advance of technology or by the liberalization of a market, for example. We live in an increasingly uncertain age and no company can afford to take for granted its survival and growth. This chapter is designed to get you to think more clearly about the nature of competitive advantage, about what makes for a sustainable competitive position and how, as the end point of the strategy process, the organization can seek to position itself in such a way that it is best able to meet the changes in the environment and to sustain itself in the face of intensified competition.

STRATEGY AS FIT

Classically, strategy was thought of as a process of matching the strengths and weaknesses of a company's internal operations to the opportunities and threats of its external environment. Until comparatively recently many companies started this process with an evaluation of the opportunities available to them in and beyond the company's immediate markets. The assumption here was that it was the role of strategy to identify opportunities for growth and

15

profitability against which the company could then position itself to take advantage of these opportunities. This approach had many adherents and led in some cases to companies diversifying away from their core businesses in pursuit of more attractive investment opportunities elsewhere.

More recently this approach had been criticized on a number of grounds:

- If investment markets are efficient then it should be for investors who own the money to make decisions about what industries they should invest in rather than managers of companies who are paid employees.
- The experience of diversification, in particular unrelated diversification, supports the view that executives often overestimate the ability of organizations to transfer expertise rapidly from one industry to another and underestimate the resources and management time required to make such transfers successful. The financial markets now also adhere to this belief and frequently discount the shares of conglomerates like Hanson or diversified groups like P&O.
- The experience of companies who have, by contrast, elected to focus on their core businesses even when, in some cases, the industry has gone into decline, seems to support the notion that the strength of companies' internal capabilities is more influential than the attractiveness of the operating environment in determining the company's success. BOC in oxygen and Richardson, the successful Sheffield cutlery maker, are good examples of this.

We can conclude, therefore, that it probably makes more sense to identify those things that a company does well and does better than its competitors and base the strategy on this, rather than attempting to grab opportunities as they come along. None of this rules out diversification as a strategic option, but it does suggest clearly that any diversification should be based upon an exploitation of the company's internal capabilities. We shall return to this later.

Identifying your strengths

The first stage in the process is to review amongst yourselves the internal operations of the organization against the following questions:

- Do the internal aspects of our company, its structure, policies, organization, finance, etc. support the overall strategy which we are trying to pursue?
- Are these aspects of our operations a strength relative to the competition, a weakness, or are they broadly neutral?

From Resources to Capabilities

Organizations are not haphazard collections of individuals involved in discrete activities – it is the processes or routines which underpin organizational life which often yield competitive advantage. These processes may be internal: for example, the way in which Japanese companies have adopted simultaneous or parallel processing of design and development activities in the car and electronics industry has enabled them to bring products to the market much more quickly. Equally, competitive advantage may be derived from the way in which the organization relates to its suppliers and its buyers along the industry's value chain. Thus it is well known that the introduction of 'Just-in-Time' supply methods which minimize inventory of raw materials and components in manufacturing operations is underpinned by electronic data interchange, automatic re-ordering and, more broadly, 'shared destiny' relationships between manufacturers and their suppliers.

So, in assessing your company's capabilities, take a look at the key cross-functional processes which may be in the primary production or delivery system but may also include things like product development, quality control, after-sales and invoicing, and assess the following aspects:

- Which of the links in the value chain between the different functions of the organization are sources of strength for the company?
- Which linkages with other organizations in the value chain (suppliers/buyers) can be regarded as strengths?

From capabilities to sustainable competitive advantage

So far we have established that for a company's resources to be a strength it has to be better in some way than the competition and that for strengths to form the basis of capabilities they have to be configured in ways that are not easy to imitate. This brings us to the last stage which is to the notion of sustainable competitive advantage.

In order for a company's capabilities to be a sustainable source of competitive advantage they must satisfy certain criteria:

Durability

It is commonplace that the speed of technological change is leading to a rapid depreciation in the value of many companies' fixed assets. Technological obsolescence will mean that the value of a five-year old computer, for example, would be virtually zero. Likewise, the shortening of product life-cycles and the ease with which competitors can replicate product features has eroded the specific competitive advantages to be derived from a particular product such as a new car, a new computer or a camera. On the other hand, many capabilities are of a much more durable nature. Think of the brand names of confectionery like chocolate bars or boxes of chocolate. Many of these like Mars Bar, Kit-Kat, Cadbury's Dairy Milk and the like, have been around for 50 years or more and because of high customer loyalty underpinned by continual brand promotion these products have been able to sustain their position in the market despite competition from newer products.

Rarity

Since time immemorial speculators have been aware that by restricting the supply of certain commodities, silver say, or grain, you could increase their value: where the company has access to capabilities which are rare then this can provide a source of competitive advantage. The world of professional football is replete with examples of journeyman players, but the star players are much rarer and this is reflected in their high transfer fees. Likewise, you could extend this analogy to the world of advertising, pharmaceuticals, or the stock market.

Immobility

Of course the problem with valuable assets like star football players or investment analysts is that they have a habit of walking out of the organization and taking the source of the company's competitive advantage with them! One way to circumvent this problem is to ensure that the basis of the knowledge or the expertise underpinning this advantage becomes less mobile. For example, product or market knowledge can be collated on a database which can then be appropriated by the company rather than left within the purview of any particular individual.

Inimitability

If it is easy for a competitor, having recognized a company strength, to imitate or replicate the advantage, then it is no longer sustainable. In some industries a company's position can be protected by legal means, for example, the use of patents in the pharmaceutical industry. But in other industries the ease with which companies can legally or illegally copy a product or service may mean that continuous innovation is the only way to stay ahead of the smart 'fast follower'. Inimitability is likely to be enhanced where specific historical, cultural or national characteristics underpin strengths. For example, the life time employment system which has benefited Japanese companies for much of the post-war period has enabled them to keep closer control on their sources of inimitable competitive advantage. Similarly, if it is not easy for a competitor to work out what the source of the competitive advantage is or to disentangle it from a number of potential sources of competitive advantage, then that can make it difficult to imitate.

Valuable

It goes without saying that for a strength to be sustainable it must either be valued by the customer who is paying for the product or service and/or enable the organization to reduce its costs and therefore offer a price advantage to the customer. Clearly the nature of value is a dynamic concept: what customers were willing to pay a premium for ten years ago will often no longer be a source of differentiation. Quality is a good example of this.

Substitutability

Many companies that have attained a sustainable competitive position for a long period in their chosen market place fail to see that their long-term competitive position is being eroded, not by any relative weakening in their position *vis-à-vis* their competitors, but by the emergence of substitute products or services – networks of PCs instead of mainframes for example – which can erode their position. Similarly, it is easy for companies operating in industries with no apparent substitutes to forget that further on down the value chain substitute products may well be impinging upon their competitive position. Thus the main threat for tyre manufacturers comes not from the direct substitutes for the tyre but from other forms of transport which could lead to limitations in the development of the road transport market.

The Foundations of Corporate Success

John Kay, an economist and leading writer on business strategy, has applied the notion of sustainable competitive advantage to a number of well-known companies. On the basis of his research he has identified four sources of abiding corporate success which either singly or in combination underpin successful companies:

- Innovation – defined as the capacity for the organization to introduce change in terms of its products, processes, organizational structures or policies rather than simply new product development – can be a source of sustainable advantage. The introduction of the radial tyre by the French tyre company Michelin and the development of a new process of making sheet glass by Pilkingtons are good examples of innovation as a source of advantage.
- Architecture – this refers to the way that a company configures its assets and manages the linkages between them. Thus the formation of cohesive project teams under a powerful project leader has underpinned the success of Japanese companies to bring products to the market quickly.
- Reputation – as a basis of competitive advantage reputation often flows from success in innovation and/or architecture but, to some extent at least, can enjoy an independent existence. Thus Rolls Royce motor cars enjoyed a reputation for being the world's best car long after it had been overtaken in purely technical terms by German and Japanese competitors. Reputation, which may be reflected in strong brand names, high customer loyalty and extreme price insensitivity (where customers wish to pay *more*) will ultimately be eroded if companies do not invest sufficiently in its maintenance.
- Strategic assets – unlike the other sources of advantage, which are essentially internally driven, strategic assets are those sources conferred upon a company by nature of its position within its society or business system. Thus the low cost of capital in Japan, the protection of Fiat's home market against Far Eastern competition and the barriers to entry imposed by government regulators in telecommunications markets around the world are all examples of

how strategic assets can underpin competitive advantage. Ultimately however, in a world where de-regulation, liberalisation, and mobile financial resources are increasingly the norm, such strategic assets are unlikely to form the basis for sustainable advantage.

Source: John Kay, *Foundations of Corporate Success*, Oxford University Press, 1993

USING A COMPANY'S WEAKNESSES

Wise companies recognize their weaknesses as well as their strengths. This is an often neglected part of the strategy process. Some weaknesses may be insignificant from a strategic point of view: despite the rhetoric of the quality movement no one has yet succeeded in producing the perfect organization! Organizations are a product of their members, their strengths and their natural tendencies. In order to survive and thrive organizations will place emphasis on some aspects of their operations at the expense of others. This is normal and understandable. Weaknesses can be important from a strategic point of view in the following circumstances:

- If a weakness is critical to a company's customers then it could limit the sustainability of the organization in the longer term. In a perfectly competitive market suppliers that are not able to deliver at low cost will find that this weakness may be terminal. Likewise, in areas where after-sales and support is regarded as key, the survivability of the company itself can be a key source of weakness and this can lead to a self-fulfilling spiral of doom. Small computer companies, which fail to get orders, which in turn reduces their sustainability, often suffer from this.

- If a weakness is critical to operational effectiveness, even when the company is successful in bringing products or services to the market place which are valued by the customers, the cost may be such as to erode any economic return on the investment and limit the available income for future investment. A lot of specialized firms in Germany encounter this problem.

- If a weakness is critical to key stakeholders and if some aspects of the company's operations are regarded as a weakness by key stakeholders this could also be significant from a strategic point of view. Thus, if the nature of the leadership style or the foundations underpinning the business are not well understood by the financial community this can be a critical weakness, even though the organization may, in reality, be quite sound, as Richard Branson, amongst others, has discovered in the past when trying to raise funds for expansion.

Even where weaknesses are held to be critical they may not be important from a strategic as opposed to an operational standpoint unless any of the following conditions apply.

- If the weakness is persistent and is perceived to run for some time without any serious attempt to address it, this can erode a company's competitive position.
- If the source of weakness is not easy to repair, perhaps because it exceeds the present resources of the company, then this suggests that it could be a source of competitive disadvantage. Scale disadvantages in volume industries, for example, can often be decisive and may lead organizations to contemplate acquisitions.
- Even where weaknesses are persistent and cannot easily be addressed within the existing resource base, companies may still be capable of other actions which can at least partially offset the effect of these weaknesses. So an ageing product line can be partially offset by superior after-sales service, for example. Skoda have demonstrated this: they score the highest of any European car manufacturer in customer satisfaction surveys.

ATTAINING A COMPETITIVE EDGE

At the outset of this chapter we said that it makes more sense often to build strategy on underlying core competences or capabilities rather than starting from market opportunities and working back. Where a company has a strength which is discernibly better than its competitors and can be sustained, this should provide the basis for its future competitive strategy. Such capabilities need to be protected, nurtured and exploited and we will go on to talk about how that can be done in further chapters. Where weaknesses are critical and enduring, companies should seek at the very least to neutralize them as a source of competitive disadvantage and, depending on availability of resources, even transform them into sources of competitive advantage. Where resources are limited and the weakness is likely to prove critical, then a company should think about either withdrawing from the competitive fray or bypassing the competition in some other way, for example by reconfiguring the distribution system. This was how new entrant Daewoo was able to turn a potential weakness – the lack of existing dealer bases in the UK – into an advantage, by selling direct to the end users.

EXERCISES

Now, how does this apply to your organization?

Exercise 1 Review the company's internal operations

Review the company's internal operations starting with its strategic orientation (mission, objectives and strategy) (Exercise 4 in Chapter 1). Using the grid below, rate each aspect as a strength (1–2), a weakness (4–5) or as a neutral factor (3). You may wish to subdivide the factors further. For example, 'Finance' could be 'Profitability' and 'Gearing'.

	Strength		Neutral	Weakness	
	1	2	3	4	5
Strategic Orientation					
Status (ownership)					
Structure and Style					
Management and Leadership					
Finance					
Market Orientation					
Human Resources					
Operations and Logistics					
Products and R & D					

Exercise 2 Assess strengths as sustainable sources of competitive advantage

Take all those factors you have identified as strengths (with scores of 1 or 2 in Exercise 1) and assess how sustainable they are as sources of competitive advantage. Using the grid below plot a different coloured line for each strength against the five criteria on the grid.

	HIGH				LOW	
	1	2	3	4	5	
DURABLE						TEMPORARY
RARE						COMMON
INIMITABLE						EASY TO COPY
VALUABLE						LOW VALUE
UNIQUE						SUBSTITUTABLE

Those with a profile more to the left will be sustainable sources of competitive advantage, while those to the right will be unsustainable.

Exercise 3 Assess weaknesses

Transfer the weaknesses (4–5) from Exercise 1 onto the grid below, and assess their importance against the criteria.

	HIGH				LOW
	1	2	3	4	5
Critical to customers					
Critical to operational effectiveness					
Critical to stakeholders					
Persistent					
Unrecoverable					
Cannot be off-set					

Exercise 4 Strength and weaknesses

Transfer the strengths analysed in Exercise 2 into the appropriate quadrant of the matrix below, deriving your measure of the scale of advantage from Exercise 1 (1=High, 2=Low), and the assessment of sustainability from Exercise 2 (1–2 sustainable, 3–4 unsustainable).

	Build and Sustain	Core Competence – Nurture
HIGH	1.	1.
	2.	2.
	3.	3.
	4.	4.
	5.	5.
SUSTAINABILITY		
	Harvest	Defend or Renew
	1.	1.
	2.	2.
	3.	3.
	4.	4.
LOW	5.	5.

LOW   SCALE OF ADVANTAGE   HIGH

Now transfer the weaknesses analysed in Exercise 3 into the matrix below. For example, 'lack of up-to-date plant' may be highly critical as a weakness, but is likely to be capable of being addressed. This should either be neutralized as a weakness or transformed into a strength (top right segment). By contrast, 'restricted opening hours for retailers' may be unimportant for most customers and due to cultural or legal difficulties, hard to address. The response therefore would be to hold back and monitor events.

	Withdraw or Bypass	Neutralize or Transform
HIGH	1.	1.
	2.	2.
	3.	3.
	4.	4.
	5.	5.
CRITICAL TO SUCCESS		
	Hold back and Monitor	Neutralize or Hold back
	1.	1.
	2.	2.
	3.	3.
	4.	4.
LOW	5.	5.

LOW   ABILITY TO FIX   HIGH

3 Key Success Factors: What drives business logic and how are these drivers changing?

INTRODUCTION

In the 1980s the computer giant IBM was recognized as a leader in its industry with a record of sustained innovation, growing revenues and a dominant position in the market. IBM was seen as a prime example of an excellent company lead by an excellent management. By 1994 all this had changed: IBM's market capitalization plunged, it recorded a record corporate loss and was forced into major and unforeseen changes in leadership and organization structure. What went wrong?

As we might expect no single factor explains its rapid and substantial decline. However, a significant cause of IBM's problems seemed to be its inability to adapt its 'dominant logic' in the face of dramatic changes within the industry. The development of the company in the 1980s was based on the assumption that large scale data processing was important to firms. Low volume repeat purchases of mainframe machines with highly concentrated computer power was seen as IBM's core business. But the market place at that time was changing dramatically, the late 1980s and early 1990s saw the rapid growth and development of powerful desk-top PCs. Although IBM brought the PC to the market place, its focus was still on 'mainframe' applications and it tended to deny the emerging reality of the time.

At the same time that IBM saw its market share and revenues fall, new entrants to the computer industry, like Microsoft and Dell in the US and Amstrad in the UK became successful high-growth players in this newly competitive market. They supplanted IBM in many areas that the company had seen as its stronghold without the experience, or indeed the name, of IBM on which to base their sales.

Their success shows the need to understand the logic that drives your business and anticipate changes as they emerge. The example of the IT industry shows how great opportunities can emerge from new directions in an industry or in a sector. In the first part of this chapter we will look at some key success factors that are important in many industries. This information should equip you to ask questions of your own industry about the major factors that drive the logic of your business.

In the second part of the chapter we focus specifically on key success factors for medium-sised businesses and review the results of research to date. You should then be in a position to assess your company against the characteristics identified.

The Dominant Logic

The dominant logic is the set of assumptions which people in an organization share about how the business works and what it takes to succeed in the industry. For example, there may be firmly entrenched beliefs in the business about how large the firm must be to survive or how vertically integrated its operations should be. There may be a prevailing view that the future will belong to a particular technology, as was the case in IBM.

The dominant logic is generally born out of success: the recipe that worked in the past forms part of the mental framework. Since in most companies the people who get to the top where strategic decisions are made are associated with this recipe, it can become very difficult to shift. Nothing fails like success, it is said: meaning that companies with a successful recipe find it difficult to change the dominant logic even though the logic of the industry may have been transformed out of recognition. Denial is a common response to such a situation and crisis is often the only catalyst for reassessing the dominant logic.

In the first part of this chapter we consider some key strategic concepts which influence the logic of an industry. They include the position on the life cycle, the size of the firm and its relative market share.

THE LIFE CYCLE

A key aspect of industry is the maturity of the industry or position on the life cycle. The life cycle is a durable concept probably because it mimics the life cycle of nature where we have periods of childhood, youth, maturity and decline. The pattern can be depicted on a so-called 'S-curve' (see Figure 3.1). The curve can be divided into four phases: embryonic, growth, maturity and decline. Most industries can be positioned somewhere along this life cycle, in some industries indeed it is possible to segment the industry further. The computer industry provides us with a good example of this. See if you can place the following segments of the computer industry on the life cycle model: mainframe, pen-based, desktop and laptop.

Well, as of 1997, you would probably have positioned pen-based computers in the embryonic stage. Not only is the technology still evolving, but the market for this product still needs to be established outside of a rather narrow range of technical users. It is a question not just of innovating but building credibility. Once these two things can be achieved there is a strong likelihood of exponential growth. This is happening in laptop or portable computers, the fastest growing segment in the computer industry. Not everybody yet has a portable computer and many consumers are waiting until the price is driven down still further or the power of the computers increases. The key to success here is building volume quickly and establishing

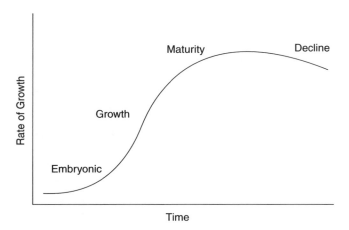

Figure 3.1   The life cycle

product and market leadership. Desktop PCs on the other hand were a major growth segment in the 1980s, they are still growing – mainly as a result of increases in processing power leading consumers to upgrade their equipment – but the market is much more mature than it was and growth rates have started to slow down. Price levels and margins have also dropped dramatically, as has the level of differentiation between the players, so that achieving cost reductions becomes imperative. Mainframes remains a lucrative market for some well-established players. It is now definitely in decline, however. Processing tasks which were previously the province of mainframes and other large computers are now being executed by networks of PCs operating with much more powerful processors.

Where would you place your industry on this industry life cycle? Is it likely that your industry will proceed through the life cycle in the same pattern as the computer industry? Some industries which have previously matured or even declined, like bicycles or watches, can be rejuvenated or de-matured by a change in consumer taste, a clever marketing idea or the emergence of new technology.

Despite the difficulties in applying the concept in reality, the life cycle can provide some useful insights, particularly about the nature of competition in industries. Thus, you would expect during the embryonic phase that there would be relatively few buyers but also a relatively small number of competitors. Competition often revolves around the functionality of the product.

As we enter into the growth phase, the growth in the market and the potential for profit will often be spotted by potential new entrants or competitors from other segments. This will intensify competition and the race to establish industry standards and dominate distribution channels will be on. Still, however, it is likely that demand will outstrip the available supply.

In the late growth and mature phase of the life cycle customers will have become more familiar with the products or service – and will be more selective and sophisticated in their consumption. Many more competitors may well have entered the market and will be trying to undercut the existing competitors to achieve the volumes that they need. Price competition will become pervasive. Eventually, the available supply will outstrip demand; established providers who are not able to adapt to the new environment and weaker new entrants may well find themselves forced out of the industry or subject to mergers or rationalization as a result of this shake-out.

By the time the industry has become mature and growth has flattened off, all the buyers who are going to buy the product have probably already made their purchases. So repeat purchases and customer loyalty becomes essential, as does reducing the cost of production in order to maintain market share.

In the decline phase demand for the product or service will fall off as consumers are attracted to other newer or more suitable products. Some competitors may exit the market at this stage, some may be swallowed up by other stronger players. These players will then move to secure a solid position within this declining market, for example by integrating forward to control their own distribution network. As the products or services are old in this phase and do not require a great amount of investment, this strategy can actually prove quite profitable as it succeeds in mopping up all the residual purchasing power for a particular product.

ECONOMIES OF SCALE AND THE EXPERIENCE CURVE

Economies of scale are a measure of the importance of absolute size to business success.

In most industries there are advantages to being big. You can negotiate cheaper rates for energy and raw materials: your cost of capital will probably be lower; you will be able to develop a more specialized work-force with higher productivity and you can spread fixed costs over a larger volume. So it pays to be big – but only up to a point. Organizations that exceed that point find they suffer from diseconomies of scale: excessive borrowing; lack of responsiveness to market trends and inertia in the face of change. This is why some quite large businesses often break up their organizations into smaller, more manageable units.

How do you know at what point economies of scale are likely to give way to diseconomies? Well, in reality it is more likely to be a range of volumes above what is technically known as minimum efficient scale (MES). This is the number of units of production you have to make to benefit from all the cost advantages of scale.

So, if you are a volume producer of motor cars you need plants that make some 200,000 units a year to be competitive on cost grounds alone. Of course, this does not mean that if you cannot sell that many cars you cannot compete. The Morgan Motor Company has managed

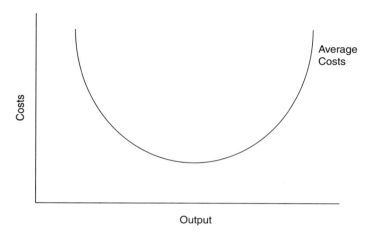

Figure 3.2 Economies of scale

for years on volumes which are much lower. But that is because the company is not competing in the mass automobile market – rather it seeks to produce craftsmen-built products tailored to precise customer specifications. Were Morgan to compete with Ford it would have to increase its volume to survive.

If you know the minimum efficient scale in your industry you can also work out how many competitors the market will bear. By dividing total market size by MES you should get a good idea of the potential competitor profile. So industries like construction or shoe manufacturing, which can operate efficiently from a relatively small scale, are characterized by many competitors and fragmented markets. At the other extreme the market for supersonic jet airlines will probably only support two or three competitors world-wide because economies of scale are critical. Be aware, however, that MES can change over time. In the 1960s and 1970s MES increased dramatically in some industries only to fall again in the 1980s and 1990s as new flexible production techniques meant that shorter runs and smaller plants were feasible.

Operating costs may be sensitive to scale, but they can also respond to increases in cumulative volume over time. This is the experience curve concept. How many times have you heard somebody refer to a 'steep learning curve' or the process of 'going down the learning curve' with a new organizational innovation? Well, the experience curve is a development of the learning curve. The phenomenon has been observed for many decades although the original scientific work was done by the US Air Force in the 1920s. The essence of the experience curve is the relationship between the volume of output of any particular good and the costs of producing it (Figure 3.3). The Boston Consulting Group, which elevated the experience curve to a major tenet of strategy in the 1960s and 1970s, did extensive studies of the application of the experience curve across a number of different industries and sectors.

They found that the experience curve effect was variable: some industries which had complex assembly operations had very pronounced effects. Others, like extractive industries or pure research, exhibited less steep curves. On average they maintained that every time output doubled costs fell 15–20%. Why should this be so? Some of it is due to static economies of scale, to be sure. But principally the benefits come from people and organizations learning to do things better and more efficiently the more often they do it.

The Boston Consulting Group, in developing the experience curve as a strategy concept, majored heavily on the linkage between market share and profitability. The logical chain went like this: dominate the market by achieving a high relative market share; this will

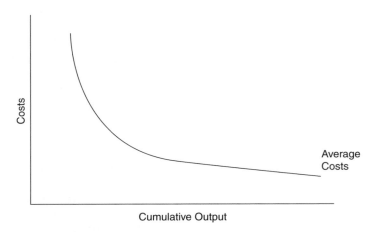

Figure 3.3   The experience curve

generate higher volumes than your competitors and enable you to achieve a lower cost position; lower costs enable you to price below your competitors and/or get superior returns for your investors; this in turn enables you to increase your market share still further at your competitors' expense: thus, a virtual circle is established.

In a world where mass consumer goods were in demand and consumers were less sophisticated this calculation in fact seemed plausible to a lot of companies. Indeed you can see it reflected in the strategies of companies like ABB, Unilever and General Electric who always aim to be number one or two in every industry they are in.

Perhaps the most famous example of an experience curve strategy at work actually pre-dates the Boston Consulting Group. This is the case of the Model T Ford. Everybody knows the story of the Model T Ford: you could get it any colour you wanted as long as it was black! Henry Ford, who was one of the earliest proponents of mass production technology, produced millions of Model T vehicles, with some body variants but all from the same basic chassis, over a period of about twenty years. In the process he drove down the cost of automobile production and transformed the car from a luxury item for the well-to-do to a mass consumer durable – arguably one of the most profound technological and social changes of the twentieth century.

Ironically, the Model T Ford also exemplifies some of the problems of relying solely on the experience curve as a strategic weapon. The Ford Motor Company demonstrated the truth of the saying that 'nothing fails like success'. Ford found it very difficult to change his initial strategy. Long after the market had become established and segmented and consumers had become more sophisticated and discerning Ford persisted with the production of the Model T. In the process he nearly bankrupted the company. Ford's major competitor, General Motors, spotted the change more quickly and was able to adapt a product range to suit the emerging segments in the market place. It stole a march on Ford which, to this day, Ford has not been able to recover.

The experience curve, therefore, can guarantee so-called first mover advantages to companies that are prepared to invest early on in a particular product or process, but only up to a point. If the choice of technology is the wrong one, or is not accepted by the market place, (as was the case with the Betamax video format, for example), if the learning effects are not proprietary and can easily be imitated by competitors who can then enter at a lower cost position; or if a newer technology can give competitors a steeper learning curve, then the experience curve will not secure a firm's competitive position.

More recently, the basic concept underlying the experience curve, the relationship between market share and profitability has been called into question by work carried out by the Stanford Research Institute in their PIMS (Profit Impact of Market Strategy) Database. PIMS records data from several thousand companies and tries to draw correlations based on regression analysis between the strategies that they pursue and their market performance. The PIMS data does support the position that there is a strong correlation between market share and profitability. Market leaders do tend to have superior profitability. However, not having market leadership does not automatically consign companies to low profitability. PIMS believes that the BCG argument probably exaggerates the benefit of experience curve effects. In the 1980s and 1990s PIMS maintained that the most important determinant was quality. High perceived quality relative to competitors' offerings would allow companies, PIMS maintained, to increase their relative market share and/or secure a higher price, this in turn would result in a lower relative cost through the experience curve, and a higher profitability. Market share, they believed, was a reward for higher quality and they cautioned against strategies aimed at headlong pursuit of market share at the expense of profitability. The message was clear: market share should be earned and not bought.

Despite these cautions, however, we should note that the experience curve is alive and well and has wide applications across industry. It is used in industries like the aircraft industry for working out the likely break even points on new aircraft projects which are, as you might imagine, extremely susceptible to experience curve effects. Equally, Japanese manufacturers who are operating shared destiny type relationships with suppliers will often grant exclusive supply contracts to a particular supplier, guaranteeing a long production run in return for a share of the experience curve savings. The Japanese angle, indeed, reminds us not only that experience effects still work but also that they are not automatic. Structuring yourself as an organization for learning and continuous improvement as many Japanese companies have done is likely to drive companies more quickly down the experience curve than relying on unsystematic and unprogrammed experience. This, in turn should result in a lower relative cost through the experience curve and a higher profitability.

What does this mean for small and medium-sized companies? We can't all be IBM, Boeing or Microsoft, dominating large industries and benefiting from vast scale advantages. But medium-sized companies can achieve commanding shares of niche markets and industry segments. Thus in the IT field, dominated by Compaq and Hewlett Packard, Britain's Psion has a commanding position in the palmtop computer market, whilst France's Business Objects, founded only in 1990, has a third of the world market for database-query programmes. As the next section makes clear, medium-sized companies, like the engineering companies which populate Germany's famed 'Mittelstand' can, by focusing on defendable market niches, build sustainable competitive positions.

EXERCISES

Exercise 1   Industry logic

Use the following checklist of generic determinants of industry logic to assess the main factors that seem to be driving your industry.

Base this excercise on data derived from sources *external* to the management team, like: analysts, market reports (see Chapter 11), suppliers, customers, partners, trade journals, people in branches or subsidiaries.

	Less Important	More Important
SIZE: Market growth Market share Operating economies of scale Experience curve advantages First mover advantages Vertical integration Cost effective production systems		

continued

	Less Important	More Important
DIFFERENTIATION:		
Product or service features		
Product or service performance		
Product or service quality		
Product or service diversity		
Service		
Customer loyalty		
Distribution		
Flexibility of production systems		
INNOVATION:		
Frequency of new product development		
Product standardization		
Proprietary technology		
Use of JIT		
Lean organization structures		

On this basis, how would you characterize your industry's logic now and how it might be in five years' time, by completing these statements:

- In order to survive in this industry we need to . . .
- In five years time, in order to survive in this industry we will need to . . .

Exercise 2   Dominant logic

Now think about your own organization. Get the management team to complete the dominant logic inventory from the point of view of your organization.

	Less Important	More Important
SIZE:		
Market growth		
Market share		
Operating economies of scale		
Experience curve advantages		

continued

	Less Important	More Important
First mover advantages Vertical integration Cost effective production systems		
DIFFERENTIATION:		
Product or service features Product or service performance Product or service quality Product or service diversity Service Customer loyalty Distribution Flexibility of production systems		
INNOVATION:		
Frequency of new production development Product standardization Proprietary technology Use of JIT Lean organization structures		

Mind the Gap
Now ask:

- Is there a gap between the general view of what it takes to succeed in this industry and the organization's view?
- Is there a gap between what it will take to succeed in the future and the organization's current view?

If the answer to either question is yes, you may need to consider how to realign yourself to close the gap.

4 Strategies for medium-sized companies: Lessons from the research

WHAT IS A MEDIUM-SIZED COMPANY?

Size is relative. A large player in the construction industry would be considered only to be a medium-sized player in the pharmaceutical industry and even the largest pharmaceutical companies would find themselves dwarfed by the large oil, automobile, or aircraft companies. Definitions of medium-sized companies are therefore problematic – sometimes the research defines them in terms of the number of employees (variants of between up to 100 and 500 employees being common). Another common criterion is annual sales turnover: one British study for instance, has defined medium-sized as having a turnover between £10m and £100m in the 1980s rising to £500m turnover in the 1990s.

Whilst it may be difficult to define what a medium-sized company is, it is not that difficult to tell what it isn't. So we are not here talking about the archetypal, multinational, multidivisional companies, whose products span a number of sectors, often under a common global brand, competing in mass markets. Nor are we talking about very small companies, be they start-ups or mature family businesses, often service based, serving well-defined local markets. Medium-sized companies can be found in virtually every sector of the economy, in service and in manufacturing, and they are frequently first or second tier suppliers to large companies. A medium-sized company has been memorably described as 'the company in the middle'. According to a leading expert on the subject:

It faces distinct disadvantages and yet possesses special advantages in its business operations, it has survived the initial struggle to become established and has the potential to move into the ranks of the larger nationally or internationally dominant business. It is the 'company in the middle', vulnerable having become more visible to competition than when it was unimportant and relatively sheltered by the specialist niche and yet lacking the strength of the large company gained through economies of scale.'

(Taylor et al. 1990)

The very assets which make up a medium-sized company's prime source of competitive advantage (its focus upon a particular market niche or sector) may also be its greatest weakness, exposing it both to competitive onslaught from larger players as well as the exigencies of the business cycle.

Successful medium-sized companies have always formed the bedrock of continental economies like Germany and Italy. The evidence suggests that in the eighties and nineties high-growth medium-sized companies also contributed disproportionately to economic growth and the growth of employment in the UK (Taylor *et al.* 1990). In 1990 there were over 70,000 small and medium-sized companies in the UK, but only just over 300 that could be classified as successful high-growth medium-sized companies (Emin 1990) Despite the creation of large numbers of new businesses in the UK in the last 15 years, few have grown to the point at which they are significant international players. To quote two recent researchers on the subject 'for the great majority of SMEs in the UK long term growth remains the exception rather than the rule' (Hay and Kamshad 1994) If growth and survival as a medium-sized company is so difficult it would seem unlikely that this growth comes about through accident, and indeed one of the findings from the research is that successful medium-sized companies have become successful *by design*.

Successful medium-sized companies have strategies but not necessarily plans

The link between strategic planning and business success is still contentious: many attempts have been made to find correlations in general (Pearce *et al.* 1987) and more specifically in smaller companies. There *is* evidence to suggest a positive association between strategic planning and success in medium-sized companies (Schwenk and Shrader 1993), although admittedly the benefit may be outweighed by the effort involved unless a company is in a particularly competitive industry where small differences can determine whether a company survives. Similarly Powell (1992) believes that the impact of strategic planning on company performance is likely to be greatest in those sectors where strategic planning is not widely disseminated. The evidence suggests that successful companies do not simply import strategic planning with all its ramifications: plans *per se* do not seem to lead to better performance, but the effort of planning is usually evidence of a consistent and coherent approach to the business (Bracker *et al.* 1988).

Successful medium-sized companies exhibit focus and consistency

Most studies of successful medium-sized companies indicate the importance of focus and strategic coherence. This generally means focusing on a particular product market segment and a particular set of customers, although there are national differences of approach. In Taylor's study of British and German companies it emerged that British medium-sized companies tended to focus on mature markets with low barriers to entry, whilst their counterparts in Germany preferred growth markets which they defended by investment in technological innovation and close links to their main customers. (Taylor *et al.* 1987)

The research into German 'Mittelstand' companies carried out by McKinsey is particularly interesting since Germany has so many strong medium-sized companies, notably in the engineering field (McKinsey 1993). This study set out to differentiate successful from less successful medium-sized companies and identifies simplicity as the main overarching success factor. Successful companies in terms of profitability and growth are more focused, with fewer products – (each of which has a higher volume) – fewer larger customers and a significantly reduced number of suppliers. These companies have also simplified their management by focusing on a few performance targets. As part of their policy of strategic focus they avoid mixing mass and speciality products and focus only on those products and customers that are either significant currently or could be important in the future. In the successful companies the product market focusing was part of a conscious decision and not simply a defensive response, retreating into ever smaller niches when faced with larger customers. Rather, German companies try to focus their efforts on achieving 'breakpoints' in customer functionality. A classic example is the technological breakthrough which enabled photographs to be processed and returned within one hour, as opposed to three hours or one week.

In addition to narrowing the business scope, successful German companies have also concentrated on the part of the value chain where they can create most value. They rigorously outsource, but from strength not from weakness: parts of the process which can give them competitive advantage are retained within the organization and not contracted out. Similarly, these companies have radically reduced the number of suppliers, even to the extent of single supplier relationships, and have involved the suppliers more closely in the design and production of their products.

The strategic focus is also in evidence in research and development, for successful German companies spend less overall on R&D but more per product than their less successful counterparts. It follows that they are also able to bring their products to the market more quickly and often at a lower cost than their competitors.

The importance of focus and coherence is also echoed in research done in the United States by Covin and his colleagues. (Covin and Slevin 1989; 1990). This very extensive research concluded that success was associated with an internally consistent set of strategic decisions and a focused strategy content, rather than employing random, disjointed or diverse approaches. High performing companies exhibited internal consistency and a coherent integrated competitive strategy based on the development and exploitation of distinctive competencies. (Hogg 1993).

Business focus is clearly linked to the avoidance of diversification as a business strategy, this is particularly the case in German companies. Successful medium-sized companies in the UK often compete on the ability to move in to closely related fields, either through acquisition or through franchising. This portfolio management approach is rarely exhibited by their counterparts in Germany.

Successful medium-sized companies can compete on differentiation or cost leadership

Successful medium-sized companies can compete on differentiation *or* cost leadership. Intuitively it might be argued that medium-sized companies could only compete effectively on the basis of differentiation. Certainly the studies done by Taylor and his colleagues over many years in the 1980s and 1990s seem to support this (Taylor *et al.* 1990). Such companies, it is argued, survive either by investing heavily in developing technological expertize in their chosen fields or by being extremely flexible and responsive to the needs of their customers. However, many companies, particularly in Germany, are finding that differentiated products alone will not enable them to compete effectively against the onslaught of mass customization from Japan. The successful companies in the McKinsey study pursued competitive strategies that were based upon cost leadership *and* product and service differentiation *and* time to market (McKinsey *et al* 1990: 173). It was striking that the successful companies in the study tended to be better than their competitors on all three counts, but were usually outstanding on one particular dimension. Thus in machine tools, where all competing products have a similar functionality, the successful companies achieved competitive advantage through their low-cost production and flexibility. In an era of flexible manufacturing and lean production techniques, medium-sized companies should be capable of competing not just on the basis of providing specialized goods and components but doing so at a cost that will make it worthwhile for larger companies to outsource to them (Harrison and Taylor). Covin and his colleagues in the States also found that smaller firms tended to seek growth through both cost leadership and differentiation strategies (Covin and Slevin 1990).

Medium-sized companies attain cost leadership in very different ways, however. New evidence from the United States suggests that successful medium-sized and smaller companies use output flexibility as a key strategic weapon (Feigenbaum and Karnaney 1991). This means that instead of going for economies of scale from large volume which large companies typically do, medium-sized companies rely more on labour than on capital and on variable rather than fixed costs of production. This allows them more readily to vary output in response to changes in demand.

Whether or not a differentiation or cost leadership strategy is likely to be appropriate will also depend on the company's position within the value chain. This suggests that focus differentiation strategies, based on product enhancements, are likely to be most appropriate near the end of the value chain, close to the end user. Firms successfully combining quality with price in competition with larger competitors will by contrast tend to predominate at earlier stages in the value chain. Interestingly, research from the United States suggests that a broad based strategy based on aggressive pricing *is* a feasible option for smaller companies in the earlier stages of their development, when they are able to compete without attracting retaliation from larger players. This strategy is most in evidence near the beginning or middle of the supply chain where the products supplied tend to be commodities and where upstream companies frequently push the product through the supply chain (Carter *et al.* 1994).

Successful medium-sized companies are purposeful and aggressive

The evidence from the United States, in particular, suggests that successful high-growth companies in competitive markets have both an entrepreneurial strategic posture (i.e. are not fundamentally risk averse) and have a long-term growth-orientated approach. It is not suprising that the desire to expand and be successful is associated with successful high growth medium-sized companies. The research suggests this is a necessary but not a sufficient feature, for as Kobin points out, an entrepreneurial growth orientated approach needs to be combined with a coherent strategy to achieve high performance (Covin 1991).

Successful medium-sized companies compete in a variety of different industry sectors

Globally, medium-sized companies can be found in a range of different industries. In the United States successful medium-sized companies have grown up in high tech sectors like IT and biotechnology. In the UK successful medium-sized companies have, by and large, eschewed these areas because of the high investment entry barriers or the uncertain rewards of investing in leading edge technology. Conceivably, this also reflects the greater availability of venture capital in North America than in the UK. Perhaps not surprisingly, the emphasis amongst medium-sized companies has shifted since the late 1980s in the UK. Then medium-sized companies were disproportionately present in the burgeoning property market. In the 1990s such firms were predominantly in service industries.

Successful medium-sized companies structure themselves and manage themselves in ways which encourage focus and flexibility

In Bernard Taylor's pathbreaking Anglo-German study he talks of top managers in both countries sharing a well defined 'theory of the business' coupled with so-called 'bus ticket controls': an understanding of the key financial and operating ratios which were critical to their businesses (Taylor *et al.* 1990). Striving for simplicity in the expression of objectives and their communication within the company seems to be a common hallmark of such companies. Such companies typically avoid complicated measurement systems which absorb effort and time in favour of simple, clear, delegated objectives. This is also reflected in the structure. According to McKinsey's study of medium-sized companies in Germany (McKinsey *et al.* 1993), successful companies eschew functional or matrix structures in favour of organizations arranged around business units or product groups. Each business unit in turn is treated as a profit centre or, where there is no genuine external market, as a cost centre. In less successful companies, financial control is exercised through the budget. This organizational principle of separation and delegation of responsibility is reflected widely within such organizations: for example, responsibility for quite large capital investment decisions is often decentralized. Similarly, responsibility for products is devolved to plant level. As a result feedback loops can be short and production processes can be adjusted to take account of local conditions.

Successful medium-sized companies overcome the obstacles to success

There are many obstacles for successful medium-sized firms to negotiate. Medium-sized companies are often more vulnerable to fluctuations in the business climate than their larger counterparts. This is partly because of their size and resource base, and also because frequently they are focused on one business sector. Successful firms often take refuge in relatively benign environments where customers are less price sensitive, capital is more easily available and competition is not so intense (Covin and Slevin 1989). The sheltered niche (Todd and Taylor 1992) is one way in which companies seek to isolate themselves from the vagaries of the business cycle.

Resource constraints are also commonly cited as obstacles to success. There are many famous examples in recent times of companies which have grown rapidly and ultimately exceeded their financial resources. The result is cash flow problems frequently leading to crisis and liquidation. UK companies have particular problems as regards financing (Todd 1993). On the one hand getting support from banks is much harder than elsewhere in Europe, on the other hand the stock market in the UK, particularly for smaller companies, is much more highly developed than elsewhere in Europe. The British system can push medium-sized companies into a dangerous dilemma: in order to grow they have to resort to capital markets to obtain funding, but the demands of the markets put pressure on companies to increase their profitability and dividend payments, thus discouraging reinvestment for growth. This, in turn, can also make medium-sized companies more vulnerable in the UK in the sense that information about their business operations is widely known. This contrasts with the situation in continental Europe where many medium-sized companies are still family owned (Kets de Fries 1996).

In order to survive and grow, medium-sized companies have to strike a balance between caution and aggression. Too conservative a financial policy, for example as regards debt, can lead to a risk-averse posture with minimal investment in the future. Such companies are then often condemned to retreating into ever smaller niches in order to survive. The other extreme, too expansive a policy, can lead to the financial problems referred to above. Faced with this dilemma, successful companies like the ones mentioned in the Todd and Taylor study (1993) generate as much capital as possible from within their own operations.

Faced with scarcity of finance, successful companies are often creative in finding ways of reducing capital and investment needs, for example by using relationships with large customers to reduce the risks and cost involved in launching new products. Alternatively, they may grow by relying on external capital provision, for example by leasing or franchising. Similarly acquisitions of other companies are often funded by shares in the existing companies coupled with 'earn-outs' (Todd and Taylor 1993:75).

Contrary to conventional wisdom, successful medium-sized companies often overcome the boundaries of size and limited technical and management resources through acquiring other companies. Research into the international strategies of UK medium-sized companies indicates that acquisition was a favoured strategy for expanding into Europe. Acquisitions are often preferred because they take less time than organic growth, although paradoxically successful companies spend considerable time (9 months to 2 years is typical) getting to know the potential target before the acquisition is made. Almost invariably, acquisitions by successful medium-sized companies are done on the basis of consent. The target company's track record of success, an experienced management team and a business philosophy which fitted with that of the acquiring company are commonly used as yardsticks. (Hughes 1990)

To summarize, successful medium-sized companies:

- think ahead strategically, even if they do not have a formal strategic planning system;
- are usually successful by design, not accident;
- emphasize focus, simplicity and coherence;
- can compete on cost or differentiation;
- are not exclusive to any sector or industry;
- have flexible organizational structures;
- learn how to overcome the barriers to success.

These are the findings which we will have to keep in mind as we consider the future strategy and how we implement it.

5   *Understanding the Economy*

All predictions are hazardous – 'especially those about the future'. It is easy to get the impression that forecasters always get their predictions wrong. Looking at scenarios it is striking that often even the worst-case scenario is far too optimistic when reviewed in hindsight. There are many examples we can think of when forecasters consistently got the timing or magnitude of a change in the economic environment quite wrong. In the late eighties the boom and bust cycle of the time was consistently predicted wrongly by the experts. How many times in the early eighties did building societies predict an imminent recovery in the house market only to be proved wrong? The oil shocks of the late seventies and early eighties also wrong footed our domestic and global economies as they brought economic growth to a standstill.

WHY BOTHER TO SPEND TIME TRYING TO FORECAST THE ECONOMIC ENVIRONMENT?

Many large organizations such as Shell, ICI and governments do spend significant resources in building models to predict trends and directions in the economy. There is a wealth of information available, literally daily, to inform you about prospects and key changes likely in the short and medium term.

So as not to become overwhelmed by all of this information, as a small and medium-sized business you need to be clear about which are the important variables that impact on your business and this will enable you to monitor and act on likely changes as they occur.

The most regularly available data are forecasts for key economic variables such as growth, interest rates and exchange rates. But before using these projections, how reliable are they?

The problem with economic forecasts is their reliability, or at least perceptions of their reliability. Like predicting the weather, the accuracy and reliability of economic forecasts have improved greatly in recent years, but people remember the errors and mistakes more than they do the many correct predictions.

Economic forecasts can provide a range of indicators that you can monitor to update your views as you track the actual path of the economy and its impact on your business. They can provide a framework for contingency planning and improved risk assessment in preparing alternative business strategies.

But how can you make use of forecasts when they appear shrouded in technical mystery and incomprehensible jargon? The keys to understanding and making use of economic forecasts are to:

- recognize that they are a mixture of econometric modelling and social, economic,commercial and political judgement. They are probability statements about the future that are subject to revisions;
- be aware that forecasts are made up of a single 'most likely' prediction within a cluster of alternative outcomes;
- develop a range of probable outcomes and associated scenarios in building your plans then update your views as new information becomes available.

Over time, it becomes relatively simple to keep track of the key growth indicators that are relevant to your business. You may need some initial advice on what you should monitor, and will continue to need updates on forecasts perhaps subscribing to one or more of those published. The benefits that flow from greater economic intelligence will soon outweigh the costs in time and effort of its collection.

Forecast Reliability

Technically, the primary difficulties in making good forecasts are in selecting the underlying econometric model and then collecting reliable data to input to the system.

The UK Treasury produces a monthly summary of forecasts from over 40 forecasting institutions. The models on which they are based contain many hundreds of functional specifications covering how each element of the economy operates. Each will reflect often subtle differences of opinion about the interaction of macro economic forces. For example, different views will be held by forecasters on the relative importance of monetary and fiscal policies in determining economic growth. But there is significant consensus on how the economy should be modelled. While academic institutions develop a reputation in support of specific theories, forecasters are more eclectic and will draw on a range of models as they seek to explain movements in economic variables.

Beneath this econometric puzzle, we are attempting to use a set of numerical values to measure a complex set of human interactions. The one exists in the virtual world of statistical indicators. The other is in the very real world of real people making decisions about their daily lives. Moreover, government statistics are themselves incomplete indicators of economic activity and are often revised after publication as mistakes are uncovered in their reporting and collation. So, the data are at times pale reflections of activity in the real economy.

Nevertheless, forecasters have become quite good at constructing models that are 'efficient' and 'unbiased' in providing reliable forecasts.

Economic forecasting is like a game of golf. An accomplished player will keep the flag in sight and move down the course towards the green. He will adjust this line as his shots move to either side of the fairway with occasional forays into the rough. Forecasting is an iterative process that improves in accuracy as more data is gathered and the forecast target is approached. Yet we sometimes act as if we expect a hole in one every time.

Having built a reliable model, forecasts can be wrong footed by shocks and uncertainty about future events. The forecaster frequently has to build in assumptions about the behaviour of economic agents before they themselves have made up their minds what they will do.

Uncertainty and Shocks

One recent uncertainty has been the behaviour of the housing market and related consumer expenditure. The 1990s recession and recovery has been hard to predict. Its depth was in some ways the downside of the massive 1980s boom. And its longevity has been due to the absence of consumer confidence. But why? Why are consumers so reluctant to spend more freely some five years past the turning point of the recession? The answer is a complex set of interacting forces. Or, to put it another way, we cannot really be sure.

Forecasts in Practice

Forecasts, then, are subject to errors – both those that are endemic and errors that are thrust upon them.

Forecasters have in the past done themselves a disservice in publishing single figure predictions with less prominence given to the clusters of values or variance of their forecasts. It is not surprising that practising business men and women take these at face value and become disappointed when they are wrong.

The National Institute of Economic and Social Research amongst forecasters has been quite innovative in moving from single point forecasts to probability ranges since November 1995. Like modern weather forecasts, these tell us the likelihood of their predictions coming to pass. This simple development is of much practical use.

The most effective way to use economic forecasts in strategic planning is to draw on a range of estimates for key variables that will impact on your business, then aggregate them producing a mean, highest and lowest projection. In other words develop up and down side scenarios.

Aggregating and incorporating a range of judgements and assumptions is just what the Government did in establishing its panel of economic advisers. While of limited statistical purity, it is wise to incorporate this diversity of views and expertise into your planning rather than have to pin your hopes on any one alternative.

Figure 5.1 shows what this may mean in practice. The graph represents the mean of a sample of recent forecasts together with their highest and lowest predictions. The picture that emerges is striking.

The peak of the current upturn in the UK seems to have passed and we appear to be entering a period of sustained, though declining, moderate growth to the year 2001. While those businesses waiting for a return to eighties style high growth seem likely to be disappointed, it is remarkable that even the most pessimistic forecast still has the UK growing by some 1% as we enter the next millennium. There is still room for a boom-bust cycle, but the stage seems set for a period of relatively stable growth. It is a view of the business cycle that is well worth taking into account for the medium term.

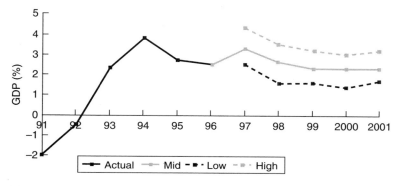

Figure 5.1 GDP forecasts 1997
Source: HMT

Inaccessibility

It is surprising how many managers are frequently unaware of key events and forecasts in the wider economy even though they can have a significant impact on their business. Perhaps this is due in some part to the inaccessibility of some forecasts and the mystery that surrounds them. If we understand better what they purport to do, economic forecasts can be useful and practical tools to the decision making and strategic management process.

EXERCISES

Exercise 1 Prospects for economic growth

We now need to take a view on the most likely prospect for economic growth over the next three to five years.

Using the 'Economy' box below, enter your view on the prospects for growth, interest rates and exchange rates in the future. Your estimate could be a single figure or a range of values.

Now do the following:

- Evaluate the impact of your growth estimate on market growth, volume and margins.
- Assess the direct impact of exchange rate and interest rates on your business.

```
┌─────────────────────────────┐
│        The Economy          │
│                             │
│  Growth:          %         │
│                             │
│  Interest                   │
│  Rates:           %         │
│                             │
│  Exchange                   │
│  Rates:           %         │
└─────────────────────────────┘
```

Business Impact

1. Cost of Borrowing (IR)
2. Competitiveness (ER)
3. Market Volumes, Shares and Margins

Market Impact

1. Market Size

2. Market Growth

Summarize your views below.

The performance of the business, given these broad economic prospects over the next three to five years, is likely to be . . .

6 Analysing the Business Environment

INTRODUCTION

Remember 9 November 1989? That was the day when, against all expectation, the Berlin wall was finally and decisively breached, and the Communist rule in Eastern Europe visibly crumbled.

Of course you could argue that the Berlin wall and the collapse of communism was an unusually dramatic change in the business environment. The fact is that few commentators up until that time had predicted the extent and the rapidity of the change. Whilst it is probably true that such 'step changes' in the business environment are becoming increasingly common, brought about by rapid rates of innovation, wholesale deregulation and unpredictable political systems, even incremental or gradual change in the business environment can bring with it profound implications for businesses. For example:

Consider the impact of the following:

- Growth rates that are higher than expected.
- Interest rates which rise to levels which are not anticipated.
- The take-up of new technologies which is slower than predicted.

Change and uncertainty appear to have become an enduring factor of business life. Our plans need to take a view of the future based on our best judgements and build in flexibility and contingencies that can accommodate unforeseen changes.

THE NEED TO UNDERSTAND THE BUSINESS ENVIRONMENT

What makes strategic decisions different from all the other decisions we have to take within organizations? There are at least two significant distinctions:

- Strategic decisions relate to the business environment outside the direct control of the organization.
- Strategic decisions relate to where the organization is going in the future.

Since our understanding of the workings of the business environment is likely to be imperfect at best and our ability to predict the future will be constrained by the many uncertainties of the business environment, this presents us with a major problem. However you cut it, this is one of the main dilemmas that all companies face with strategy. On the one hand we must make commitments, such as investment decisions, which have long-term paybacks. On the other hand, our ability to control and forecast events in the business environment is strictly limited.

However, this need not be a source of despair. We can improve strategy making by taking a more systematic approach to analysing the business environment and by adapting our approach to strategy according to the nature of the environment.

Analysing Environmental Uncertainty

It is almost a cliché that the business environment is becoming ever more turbulent and unpredictable. From an historical point of view it is not clear that the 1920s or the 1930s were any less turbulent than the 1980s or the 1990s. However, with our foreshortened historical perspective, it is probably true to say that in most businesses the levels of uncertainty today are higher than they were say in the 1950s the 1960s or the early 1970s. Why is this the case? Well of course each period has its own particular area of uncertainty. We no longer quake quite so much at the possibility of a massive rise in oil prices brought about by the whim of the OPEC Oil cartel, for example. Neither do we live in fear of a major nuclear confrontation between East and West. Instead we have new uncertainties to cope with: the myriad, smaller wars, civil disturbances and outbreaks of terrorism around the world which, at any time can be stoked up into a major conflagration as happened, for instance, in the Gulf War. We also have to cope with far greater and far more rapid changes in technology than was the case even a decade ago, as product life cycles become much shorter and technologies converge across traditional industry boundaries.

However, whilst these trends have certainly added to the complexity and turbulence of our environment, there are still some underlying trends that we can detect which are more stable and predictable. Later on in this section we will look, for example, at the impact of the business cycle, but it is often forgotten that demographic trends exhibit high degrees of stability and predictability. We can forecast with some degree of certainty, for example, what the size of the population and the relative weight within the population of certain age groups will be 20 or 30 years hence. The reality is that most industries will occupy a position along a spectrum from total stability, which arguably no longer exists, to complete unpredictability. One attempt to define such a scale has been made by Igor Ansoff (Figure 6.1).

Ansoff differentiates between *changeability,* which can be thought of as a measure of how easy it is to understand the environment, and *predictability,* our ability to forecast changes in the future. So, at one end of the scale where the environment is stable, business is essentially an economic activity mainly confined to national or local areas, events which occur in the environment are likely to be familiar and they will happen at speeds which are slower than our ability as an organization to respond. When we look into the future, it is likely

COMPLEXITY	National economic		Regional technological		Global socio-political
FAMILIARITY OF EVENTS	Familiar	Extrapolable		Discontinuous familiar	Discontinuous novel
RAPIDITY OF CHANGE	Slower than response		comparable to response		Faster than response
VISIBILITY OF FUTURE	Recurring	Forecastable	Predictable	Partially predictable	Unpredictable surprises
TURBULENCE LEVEL	1	2	3	4	5

Figure 6.1   Turbulence scale
Source: '*Strategic Management in a Historical Perspective*' by H I Ansoff, from *The International Review of Strategic Management* Vol. 2, No. 1. Reproduced by permission of John Wiley & Sons Ltd

that the pattern of events there will be simply recurring. At the other end of the spectrum, organizations are operating in very complex environments, often on a global scale and taking into account both economic, technological and broader socio-political issues. Any events happening in the environment are likely to be completely new and to change frequently: they are likely to occur in patterns which are totally unpredictable and at speeds which are faster than our ability as an organization to respond.

At what point on the turbulence scale is your organization located? Companies still operating in protected environments, nationalized industries for example or government agencies, might place themselves to the left of the scale, perhaps somewhere between one and two. If you are operating in industries like the pharmaceutical industry or the computer industry where the levels of innovation are very rapid and where the whole structure of industries can change within a couple of years, then you are probably placing yourself at four or above. Most organizations are probably located somewhere between two and four but with a distinct trend towards the right. Therein lies a major problem, because the more environments move towards the right the less easy it is to actually plan for the future.

Managing Environmental Uncertainty

There is no single right way to approach the problem of managing environmental uncertainty. How you do it depends very much on the type of organization you are and the industry that you are in. However, there are certain general principles that we can apply that can help you to choose an appropriate approach to managing environmental uncertainty. In Table 6.1 we have depicted three archetypal approaches to managing environmental uncertainty. For clarity it is helpful to keep them distinct, although in reality it is likely that organizations will not fit perfectly into one category or another. *Long range planning* describes the traditional approach adopted by a lot of large companies in the sixties and seventies when environments were more stable and time horizons much longer. At the other end of the spectrum lies *incrementalism* which describes an approach which is appropriate for very fast moving and unpredictable environments. Somewhere in the middle is what we have defined as *strategic management*: a hybrid approach which is becoming the appropriate mode for a lot of organizations which have

Table 6.1 Managing Environmental Uncertainty

	LONG RANGE PLANNING	STRATEGIC MANAGEMENT	INCREMENTALISM
LEVEL OF UNCERTAINTY	Low	Medium/High	High
MARKET STRUCTURE	Consolidated	Competitive	Fragmented
STRATEGIC AUTONOMY	High	High	Low
'LUMPINESS' OF INVESTMENT DECISIONS	High	High	Low
DEGREE OF STRATEGIC FLEXIBILITY	Low	Medium	High
ECONOMIES OF SCALE	Important	Less Important	Unimportant
FIRST MOVER ADVANTAGES	Critical	Significant	Less Significant
TIME HORIZON	Long	Long	Short
KEY SUCCESS FACTORS	Invest in the future. 'Insure' against risk	Invest in the future. Reduce asset specificity. Tie in customers	Reduce asset intensity Be responsive. Proceed incrementally

to resolve the dilemma of commitment to strategy in an uncertain environment.

Long range planning is appropriate where environments are stable, market structures are consolidated and industries dominated by a few large players who have high degrees of strategic autonomy enabling them to dictate the shape of the market and pricing levels. It also suits industries which are very highly capital intensive, which means that the investment decisions are likely to be taken in lumps or steps rather than in smooth increments. Strategic flexibility is likely to be low, in the sense that companies will be making investments in assets which will not easily be capable of being switched from one use to another use as market demand changes. The nature of the industry will mean that economies of scale are extremely important and that there will be critical advantages to competitors who are the first to enter a market and establish a dominant market position. Time horizons are long, which reflect the long pay back periods. In such situations there is no alternative to commitment. Companies have to invest in the future: simply delaying decisions on the grounds that there is insufficient information about the future is unlikely to be a successful approach, because of the risk that competitors will make more aggressive investment decisions. Classically, the way organizations manage uncertainty in this type of industry is to 'insure themselves', usually through diversification, i.e. not putting all the eggs in one basket, but maintaining interests either in other industry sectors or in other geographical markets.

The *incremental* mode is likely to be appropriate where the business environment is very turbulent and the market structure fragmented, with large numbers of competitors, none of whom who have a commanding market share, all jockeying for position amongst themselves. This is common for example in the construction industry and in a lot of craft-based industries and retail industries. In such situations individual players have little strategic autonomy and will not be able to set prices or define the market themselves. They will have to respond to competitive pressures and client demands. It is unlikely in such industries that companies will have to make heavy capital investments, and therefore any investment decisions can be made on a smoother basis. Where investments in assets are made, they must be adaptable to changes in the environment. Economies of scale are not the decisive element in competition and any advantages which first movers into a market can get are likely to be quickly eroded through imitation. Such industries will have a shorter time horizon. The recipe for success here is to keep a lean organization and not invest heavily in fixed assets: so leasing, out-sourcing and networking become important ways of dealing with uncertain demand. Successful organizations survive by riding with the waves. New departures in strategy occur, not through long-term plans, but by trial and error: investing a little bit, testing whether there is market demand and whether the products are successful before investing some more.

The real dilemma, however, occurs for organizations that are in the middle column: *Strategic Management*. Here organizations have to cope with high levels of environmental uncertainty whilst making long-term commitments through capital investment decisions. Market structures are 'oligopolistic', with a few players of reasonable size competing with one another. Each player will be capable of deploying its own strategy to secure its market share. High capital intensity will make for lumpy investment decisions and the advantages which accrue from being the first competitor in a particular industry are still likely to be significant. However, the use of new more flexible, production technology has increased the degree of strategic flexibility for such companies, by enabling them to produce different products from the same production line. The advantages of economies of scale are diminished: it is not necessary to concentrate production in huge plants in order to gain competitive advantages, although achieving a minimum efficient scale is still likely to be critical.

What is the recipe for companies in such industries? There is no alternative to thinking long term and investing in the future. If possible companies should seek to create their own futures, for instance by stimulating demand for new products. Intel, the chip-maker, expends a lot of effort on this. However, anything that can be done to reduce the time between making investment decisions and bringing products to the markets will significantly reduce risk. Equally, where investments in fixed assets are going to be made then they must be as flexible as possible to account for variations in demand, and products which require large R&D expenditures must be capable of subsequent adaptation. Finally, wherever possible, such organizations should seek to limit fluctuations in demand by tying in their customers. So instead of being dependent on a series of short term market transactions they should seek to establish strategic relationships with customers which stretch over a longer period of time and give greater stability of demand and predictability for investment decisions.

Analysing the business cycle

If investing in the future is part of the business logic of your company, then there is no alternative but to take a view of where the business environment is going and what the critical issues are. This means that you will have to take some view of how the economy and the business cycle is likely to impact on your business.

Some industries are extremely sensitive to fluctuations in the business cycle. Car manufacturers, for example, follow economic forecasts very closely, because they know that the level of general business activity in an economy is likely to determine the level of demand for cars. This is particularly the case within a mature industry like the automobile industry, where the manufacturers rely very much on replacement demand. In such a situation a recession is likely to delay the replacement purchase decision and a return to growth is likely to accelerate it. The construction industry is another industry where demand is dependent upon changes in the business cycle, although this may or may not be modified by government decisions to increase public expenditure on works programmes, for example. Some industries seem recession proof. The food industry is often cited in this regard, on the grounds that whether the economy is up or down people still need to eat. At the retail level it is probably true to say that food demand does not fluctuate as much as it does in other industries. However, greater disposable income can increase discretionary spending on higher value added items, including things like organic foods and specialized imports. Equally, there is a belief that possession of very strong brands can isolate companies from movements in the business cycle. The evidence on this is mixed, however. The possession of a strong brand with a powerful reputation on its own is unlikely to isolate companies from recessionary effects, unless it is associated with high levels of innovation and a consumer-oriented product policy. Contrast the impact of the 1990s' recession on Mercedes and BMW for instance: both companies had strong brands and formidable reputations, but Mercedes suffered most, mainly because its products, particularly at the top end, were perceived to be out of tune with the prevailing recessionary environment. Finally, some businesses are counter-cyclical: liquidations and video sales both benefit from a recession, for example!

How do we make sure that we are taking into account all the relevant factors to do with the business environment when we formulate our strategy? Well one of the techniques we could use is to develop a set of scenarios about the industry.

Scenarios are a way of exploring alternative visions of what the future is going to bring. You could think of it as a film script with alternative endings. Playing through the alternative scripts allows you to speculate about the impact of events on your business and to test the robustness of the strategy that you are going to adopt. So in the oil companies, which were amongst the first to pioneer the use of scenarios, they adopted a series of scenarios around the price of oil and explored what the likely impact would be if the price of oil were to increase substantially above its current price or decrease substantially.

Scenarios are useful devices and can be employed at all levels and in all sizes of companies with varying degrees of sophistication. We recommend, however, that they be done *not* at the analysis stage but later on when testing the strategic options. This is because scenarios are essentially open ended: they do not require analysts to make definitive judgements about where they think the business environment is going to go. The problem of scenarios for strategists, however, is that at some point we have to make a commitment. We have to back our hunch about where the business is going. So this is the next task we need to perform: identifying the major trends and issues in the environment and assessing their likely impact.

PEST Analysis

A useful device to help us with this process is PEST analysis; PEST is an acronym which stands for:

- Political
- Economic
- Social
- Technological

The idea is that the organization should collate as much relevant information as it can about its business environment. The sources of this type of information are likely to be very disparate. They may include: newspaper cuttings, articles from trade journals, publications from trade associations, analysts' reports, government publications, economic forecasts, corporate planning departments. A list of sources can be found in Appendix A.

But, equally, companies should be aware of the many *informal* sources of information about how the environment is going to change. This can be gleaned, for example, from the sales force, who may have information about trends in demand and competitive positioning. Attendance at conferences and functions, or informal business gatherings can help to generate sources of information which can be used in the analysis.

Start by holding a brainstorming session. Remember the rule for brainstorming: in order to ensure maximum scope for creativity there should be no rejection of suggestions in the initial round. Once you have got down as many issues as people think are relevant and important you can then group the issues under the PEST headings. Once you have done the first cut try to review the results. It may be that three or four issues that people have put down, de-regulation, competition, new entrants, for example, can be grouped together as one issue. In some cases you may feel that an issue spans more than one heading. For example, interest rate policy could be thought of as both an economic and a political issue. Ultimately, it does not really matter where you place it, the important thing is that by going systematically through the PEST framework (Table 6.2) you have included all the most significant trends and issues in the environment.

The next stage is to investigate what the likely impact is going to be. You can use Table 6.2 to help you in this process. After identifying the issue you need to describe what direction the trend is likely to move in (are we likely to see an increase or a decrease in de-regulation, for example?) and what the likely impact is going to be. We have included three categories of impact: impact on the total size of market demand, the impact on the relative size of market segments within the total demand and the impact on the type of product demanded. In each of these categories it is helpful to do some thinking about what the logical cause and effect is going to be. So, if deregulation occurs, is that likely to lead to lower prices which could stimulate demand and increase the overall market size? Even if the overall market size is increasing, however, will deregulation lead to greater cost and price sensitivity? In which case there may be a trend towards lower priced, as opposed to differentiated, goods. This might also have a knock-on effect on the type of product which is demanded: perhaps less sophisticated products that offer value for money may be more appreciated rather than the latest state of the art product.

Finally, we suggest you take some view of the overall importance of the issue. There are a couple of alternative ways of doing this. Which route you choose is very much dependent on how happy you feel with 'subjective' or 'objective' weighting schemes. You need, in any case, to take a view of both the likely impact of the particular issue and the probability that that issue will occur. These two are quite distinct: you can probably think of events which may have a very high impact upon the business environment but which are unlikely to occur. The impact of a huge meteorite hitting the earth, for example, would be extremely significant to all our businesses! But hopefully the probability of this occurring is not too high. Equally, there will be events that will have a high degree of probability but relatively low degree of impact. In some industries, for

Table 6.2 Environmental Analysis

Environmental Issue Force	Likely Trend/ Direction	Effect on Size of Market	Effect on Market Segment	Effect on Type of Product Demanded	Impact	Prob- ability	Import- ance
Political							
Economic							
Social							
Technological							

example, that may be the case with demography, where we know with high degrees of certainty what is going to happen. But it may be that the changes are so slow that they are unlikely to impact significantly upon the industry. These two taken together, impact and probability, make up what we call the importance factor. You can assess each of the issues in impact and probability as being high, medium or low. Now circle all the issues that are medium or above, underlining those that are high/high. An alternative method is to use a numerical weighting system. Define the impact of a particular issue on a scale of 1 to 5, where 1 is low impact and 5 is very high impact, and then multiply that by the probability of it occurring where 0 is impossibility and 1 is total certainty. The multiplied score will then give you a figure for importance which you can use to compare the various issues (See Table 6.3).

So, what do you do with your analysis once you have done it? Well, the first thing is that by doing this analysis you should be clearer on what the major issues in your business environment are. You may need to do more work on these issues, e.g. by gathering data together on those issues which are likely to be very important.

Once you have conducted your environmental analysis you can feed the results into your analysis of the competitive dynamics of the industry and ultimately into the opportunities and threats part of your SWOT analysis. In industries where time horizons and pay-back periods are lengthy then the chances are that your company will spend a lot of time involved in environmental analysis and may build the results into an econometric model. This is true, for example, in the case of the aircraft manufacturing industry which is known to be a data rich industry. Here pay-back periods may be ten years or more and all the major manufacturers publish twenty year forecasts of market demand on an annual basis. The benefits of long-term planning and perhaps influencing market developments through publishing these plans can far outweigh their costs.

Of course forecasts of market demand are subject to error and can vary from maker to maker. But in our experience there is greater variation in the assumptions that are made about likely market shares: as a general rule of thumb everyone thinks they are going to get a larger market share than they will in reality. This can be a problem if industry investment programmes are based on over optimistic assumptions about market share. In 1991, for example, all the major aircraft manufacturers were estimating a market demand for regional

Table 6.3 World Tyre Industry 1995–2000

Force	Issue/Trend	Direction	Impact on market size	Impact on type of product	Impact on operations	Scores		
						Impact	Probability	Importance
Political	Controls on vehicle use	Increase	reduce replacement demand		overcapacity possible	4	0.1	0.4
	US cafe regulations	tighter		demand for green tyres	adaptation of plant and process	2	0.9	1.8
	Controls on pollution	tighter	extended tyre life reduced demand	demand for re-treads	investment in in-house re-treading	4	0.7	2.8
	Control of market access	stable	reduce market development in e.g. China	demand for lower tech, locally produced tyres	need to invest in local plant	2	0.9	1.8
Economic	Business cycle	slow growth	gradual expansion pronounced in Asia	demand for lower price, longer life tyres	gradual absorption of over capacity; shift to Asia	5	0.7	3.5
	Commodity prices	stabilize	scope for lower cost stimulates demand	less demand for alternative commodities	less need for backward integration	4	0.5	2.0
	New entrants	increase		competition at low end	adding capacity	3	0.8	2.4
Social	Maturity of market	stable	gradual increase	fragmented markets emerging segments	need to produce full range and short runs	4	0.9	3.6
	Environmental awareness	increase	extended tyre life reduced demand	re-treads more acceptable	investment in re-treading and re-cycling	3	0.6	1.8
	Industrial re-structuring	continue			new working practices flexibility v paternalism	2	0.7	1.4
	Growth of 'own brands'	increase		reduce margins at low end	emphasis on low cost	3	0.8	2.4
Technology	Flexible manufacturing	increase		allow shorter runs, more niche products	need to progressively introduce to stay competitive	2	0.8	1.6
	Automation	increase			need to 'sell' to workforce and governments	4	0.6	2.4
	Product life cycle	decline		newer more advanced products	investment in R&D required	4	0.5	2.0

jet aircraft of in the region of 600–700 aircraft for 1994. However, if you added up the number of aircraft each manufacturer thought it would be selling based on an estimate of its market share this would have come to nearer 900! So there was a gap of some 300 aircraft between the likely market size and the levels of production. This leads to the problem of over-capacity. How can companies cope with this problem? It is not easy but here are some ideas:

- Bring your break even point down so that the company can survive even on the worst case projection.
- Tie in customers as far in advance as possible.
- Reduce the elapsed time between investment and return.
- Make production processes flexible.
- Build in provisions for change in the product design to respond to changed market conditions.
- Try to stimulate demand for your products by thinking of new end users.
- Think of how the industry could be restructured to eliminate over-capacity.

EXERCISES

Exercise 1   Environmental analysis

Gather together a team of people from different parts of the business to do the following (record your answers on a flipchart):

1 Brainstorm the key issues that are likely to affect your industry and your company in the forseeable future.
2 Review the issues and cluster together similar issues with common themes, for example, de-regulation, technology convergence, green issues.
3 For each theme identify the likely trend or direction of change, e.g. more or less de-regulation. Enter the themes into the PEST framework shown in Table 6.2.
4 Assess the impact of each theme on the total market size, the type of product or service demanded and the company's operations.
5 Rank the themes according to their overall relative impact on a scale of 1–5 (1 = low, 5 = high).
6 Now assess the probability of the change actually occuring in the foreseeable future on a scale of 0–1 (0 = impossible, 1 = certain).

7 Multiply the values in (5) and (6) together to produce an overall ranking of importance.
8 Highlight the most important issues and any areas where more information is needed.

This exercise will have enabled you to spot the environmental factors in your market that require the most urgent attention. You will be using this information later, when we work out the operations of strategic options.

7 Understanding Competitive Dynamics in Your Industry

INTRODUCTION

- Why is it that in the construction industry many companies cannot seem to break out of a pattern of low margins, marginal differentiation from competitors and weak customer loyalty?
- Why is it in contrast, that fast food outlets like pizzerias often seem to enjoy much higher margins?
- Why is it that small family bakeries now find it difficult to survive and generate funds for reinvestment?
- Why is it that in the late 1980s 'do-it-yourself' superstores could support many vigorous competitors, but in the 1990s the industry has experienced a massive shake-out?

All these questions illustrate the importance of industry structure and competitive dynamics. To operate successfully requires an understanding of them, the characteristics you need to survive as a medium-sized business under these conditions and how dynamics are likely to change over time.

MARKET STRUCTURES

Market structures can be classified into three types: monopoly; monopolistic competition; and perfect competition.

A pure *monopoly* is where a single firm supplies all of the output within a particular market. In practice, monopolistic industries often have one large dominant player with a number of other much smaller players selling to the same market. A good example of a monopoly is British Telecom in the UK telecoms market before liberalization. British Telecom was established as the sole UK provider of non-broadcast telecommunication. Until it was privatized it was the only company which could offer this service to UK customers. It is noticeable that even since the privatization and the general liberalization of the industry, BT has retained a very dominant position within the telecoms market with relatively minor incursions so far from companies like Mercury and some North American suppliers. Due to their dominant position in the market monopolists are often able to influence prices, restricting supply and charging a premium price to improve their level of profitability. They will often extract so-called 'super-normal profits', i.e. a rate of return in excess of what is required to keep shareholders happy.

Monopolists tend to secure their position in businesses that benefit from large scale production and the need to invest heavily in research and development. By investing in scale and by making high levels of R&D spending a prerequisite for entry into the business, monopolists are able to preserve their monopoly position by keeping new entrants out. They may also seek to protect their distribution outlets and spend relatively high proportions of their revenue on advertising. These are typical strategies for keeping potential new entrants out of the industry.

At the opposite extreme to monopolists are firms taking part in so-called *perfect competition*. These firms are not able individually to influence price or quantity supplied in the market. They are price takers, i.e. a firm will look at the price that is being supported by the market and decide whether it can provide the goods or service in demand profitably and how much it can supply. In perfect competition no firm will, in the long run, be able to make returns over and above normal profit. In the short run a firm may be able to improve its profitability by offering a product variation. However, other firms will soon spot the opportunity created and will follow its lead. Because entry into the market is free and there is easy access to technology, new entrants will find it quite easy to mimic the innovation of the more profitable business. This will mean that output will expand, prices will come down and with them levels of profitability. The theory goes on to suggest that new entrants will continue to be attracted to the industry as long as super-normal profit is being made but this will erode over time until only normal profit is made.

Finally there is *monopolistic competition*. This is really a hybrid between monopoly and perfect competition. This type of market structure is much more common than the other two kinds and is characterized by three to seven main players all offering similar products which are slightly differentiated from each other. It is this level of differentiation which is the key to understanding monopolistic competition.

If we think of the first two types of market structure, it is clear the last thing any business wants to be in is a market characterized by perfect competition! By contrast a monopoly seems to enjoy very attractive rates of return. It is likely then that businesses will try to act like monopolies, by creating a real or perceived difference between their products and those that are offered by other firms. That is to say, they will differentiate. If a firm can differentiate its product from those of its competitors it is likely to create loyalty amongst its customers. This loyalty should enable the firm to increase its prices relative to its competitors and improve its profitability. A monopolistic competitor or niche maker therefore exploits the opportunity to achieve levels of super-normal profit.

The question the niche maker then needs to ask is: is the niche defensible or will it inevitably disappear? Just as in perfect competition, achieving super-normal profits will act as a signal to other competitors to enter the niche. The niche maker can try to protect its niche by raising its differentiation, for example by investing in advertising to maintain awareness of its brand.

Alternatively the firm will have to look at other potential niches and be willing to let go of the super normal profits made in its original niche. This kind of firm must be an innovator, continually developing new products or services to sell to the market to reap the high levels of profit that it will achieve for a short period before moving to a new niche where new levels of super normal profits can be achieved. Examples of both strategies abound. Strongly branded products like Mars Bars and other chocolate bars are good examples of strategies for building and protecting branded niches. Computer companies are often seen as highly active innovators producing a new product in one year which is highly profitable and then moving on. Likewise the consumer hi-fi market is characterized by very high levels of innovation or, product churning.

Depending on what businesses do in their market and the underlying economic pressures in the industry, different kinds of market structure are thus likely to emerge which in turn will imply different kinds of competitive behaviour by players. Market structure is not a static concept. Over the life cycle of a product we are likely to see market structure changing. In the initial stages of a product introduction or a service innovation we are likely to see a monopoly open up. After a while, depending on issues such as the minimum efficient scale present in the industry and how easily technology and technological change can be replicated, we are likely to see new entrants come into the market and this may lead to a segmented market with monopolistic competition. This in turn may ultimately turn into quite an open competitive market with what was originally a very strongly differentiated and branded product becoming a commodity product. Alongside this changing pattern of market structure we will also tend to see rates of return in the industry changing over time. Initial high levels of profitability will almost inevitably decline as the product and the industry matures and eventually declines.

To put these ideas into pictures, the monopolist is often seen as the whale in the ocean of the commercial world. Whilst strong and long-lived the whale is seen as an animal which is slow to adapt to environmental changes so that if the seas increase in temperature by one or two degrees we are likely to see a decline in the population of the whale. This analogy can be applied to some of the industrial monopolies and some of the industrial giants such as IBM or British Gas who have suffered by being unresponsive to environmental change over the last decade. Monopolistic competitors are the dolphins of the commercial world. They are the players who, like Hewlett Packard, can collaborate to achieve competitive advantage yet at the same time work independently. They can act rationally but can also think laterally and creatively in responding to change and new opportunities within their world. Many organizations have been changing their ways of working to become more dolphin like. We have seen this over the last decade as firms have reduced their size to become leaner and more in touch with their customers.

There is another form of market structure called *oligopolistic* which usually involves two or three major players. This is likely to occur when an industry achieves high levels of concentration. Through mergers and acquisitions, market share is concentrated amongst two or three players all of which are of similar size. This form of competitive behaviour is quite different to that seen in other forms and can be quite unpredictable. What is clear is that the behaviour of each firm will very much be dependent on action taken by its competitors. Oligopolists will develop strategies which are partly aimed at customer needs but are also aimed at beating their opposition and maintaining their own competitive position. Examples of oligopoly are the soft drinks industry, where Coca-Cola and Pepsi Cola are in head-on competition in their global markets, or in the UK brewing industry which has been subject to a process of consolidation throughout the 1990s. To sustain the animal metaphor, oligopolists are like two or three powerful gorillas all in the same cage slowly and carefully circling each other looking for opportunities to express their competitive domination but being very aware of the moves of each other.

ANALYSING INDUSTRY ATTRACTIVENESS

So far we have established that market structures vary according to the number of players in the market and their market shares. This in turn is likely to affect the overall levels of profitability in an industry which would be a major determinant of that industry's attractiveness.

This concept of industry attractiveness has been elevated to a major focus of competitive strategy through the work of Michael Porter. Porter's thesis is that the ability of a company to make a reasonable return on its investment will be a function largely of two factors:

- the overall attractiveness of the industry;
- the success of a particular company's competitive strategy within the industry.

This second aspect will be dealt with in greater depth in Chapter 9. Industry attractiveness which we will deal with here is a function of competitive forces in an industry. Porter has developed a model for analysing these forces which is sometimes known as the 'Five Forces Model' or 'The Porter Model' (see Figure 7.1).

Most of us when we think of competition tend to focus initially on the degree of rivalry between competitors in an industry: so we think of Tesco versus Sainsbury's, General Motors versus Ford or Unichem versus AAH in pharmaceutical distribution. As we have already seen

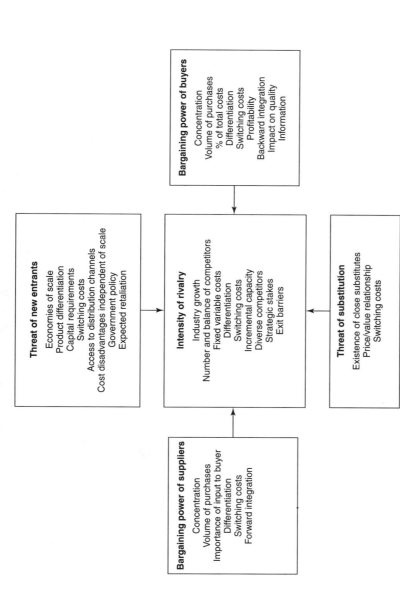

Figure 7.1   Porter's five forces model (Adapted with permission of the Free Press, an imprint of Simon & Schuster, from *Competitive Strategy: Techniques for Analyzing Industries and Competitors,* by Michael E Porter. Copyright © 1980 by The Free Press.)

rivalry can be a major factor and is likely to be in large part a function of the structure of the industry. Other factors which are important are:

- the degree of differentiation separating competitors;
- the amount of growth in the market place;
- the presence of over capacity in the industry;
- the ability of the players to withdraw from the industry if necessary (the 'exit barriers');
- the likelihood of establishing a consensus amongst the players about the rules of the game for competing.

However, rivalry is not the only driver of industry attractiveness. In most industries the threat of new entrants coming into a market place will be sufficient to limit the profitability of the players already in the market. As new entrants come into an industry, levels of profitability are likely to be reduced due to the increased competitive rivalry; therefore, existing players will seek to deter new players from entering. They may threaten retaliation, or they may try to build barriers to entry to stop new players from coming in. Barriers to entry may include:

- the capital outlay and the economies of scale which are needed to operate in the industry;
- possession of key brands;
- tying up distribution channels or sources of supply;
- possessing exclusive access to technology or know-how;
- government protection.

Even if barriers to entry are sufficiently high to protect incumbents, substitute industries may grow up capable of offering products or services to the industry's clientele with a better combination of value for money. This often occurs through technological innovation or industrial convergence, and it can exert a powerful competitive influence on the industry. See, for example, the impact of the Channel tunnel on cross-channel ferry operators.

The extent to which companies in an industry retain the profit which they generate is in large measure a function of their bargaining power *vis-à-vis* their suppliers, on the one hand, and their buyers on the other hand. In effect, they compete with these other stages in the value chain for a bigger slice of the profit pie. Thus, powerful suppliers will bid up the prices of goods or services supplied, whilst powerful buyers will exert downward pressure on the price of goods or services offered. Buyers' power is likely to be enhanced if:

- they buy a large proportion of the goods or services produced;
- there is no differentiation between products;
- there are no switching costs for buyers in changing from one producer to another;
- the producers have high fixed costs which they must cover through increasing turnover even at the expense of margins;
- they can integrate backwards if they don't like the prices they are offered.

Not surprisingly perhaps, supplier power is a mirror image of buyer power. Thus suppliers will have more power if:

- there are only a few available suppliers;
- the goods or services supplied are highly differentiated;
- the suppliers are not dependent totally on the industry;
- suppliers can integrate forwards if they do not like the price that they are getting for their services.

So each of the five forces is determined by a combination of factors, some of which may point in different directions. Usually one or two of the forces tend to be the most significant and attention can be focused on these.

There are three main ways of using the model:

1 A static analysis – this enables us to answer the question – 'Is this an attractive industry to be in?'
2 A dynamic analysis – by factoring in the results of our PEST analysis which we did in Chapter 6, we can try to assess the impact of these trends and issues on the competitive forces: thus, for example, deregulation might lead to a reduction in entry barriers and an increase in the threat of new entry.
3 Prescriptive – here the question is not so much 'what is or will be', but 'what might be'. How can companies, even quite small companies, improve the attractiveness of the industry? For example, rivalry can be reduced by restructuring an industry around fewer players and bargaining power can be offset by establishing closer, longer term collaborative relationships between buyers, suppliers and producers.

COMPETITOR ANALYSIS

Competitor analysis has now become an art form in its own right giving companies ways of generating data about competitors from formal and informal sources, analysing their actions and intentions, and even in some cases role playing their likely movements.

Some companies gather competitor data systematically; they may derive data from trade associations, commercial databases or from competitor reports completed by the sales force and other employees with a direct market interface. Leading edge companies like UPS or AT&T are now using groupware or intranet systems to capture competitor information and make it available throughout the organization. Often this information is gathered more informally, particularly in smaller organizations. But it is a good idea to make someone responsible for gathering and disseminating competitor information and feed the results of competitor analysis into the strategy process.

Start by making a comprehensive list of who your competitors are. In some industries it may be difficult to be comprehensive. In such cases make sure you choose the main competitors and also a representative selection of different types of competitors. For each competitor you can use the framework in Exercise 4 below. Start by asking what assumptions the competitor is making about the industry – to refer back to the point we made earlier in the chapter – what is the dominant logic within the competitor? Next look at the objectives, either stated or inferred, which the company has set itself. For example is this competitor going aggressively for market share or is it more interested in short-term profitability? The logical next step is to identify the strategy which the company is pursuing. This may or may not be publicized, but in any case you can look for external indications: for example, the acquisition of another company, the construction or extension of production facilities, the opening of new subsidiaries, the launching of an advertising campaign or the recruitment of new employees. Finally, you need to review what the core competences or the capabilities of the competitor are. In this context it is important to ask firstly whether the company has the wherewithal to implement its strategies successfully and fulfil its objectives and also how the company is likely to respond to any moves that you as a company might make.

One helpful technique to think through your competitors' strategy is to try to map out the industry and its competitors by what is known as strategic group analysis. This can be done graphically by choosing as the two parameters for the axis those characteristics which are most likely to differentiate the company's strategic position. It may be business scope and market position for example, or it could be degree of internationalisation plotted against the degree of vertical integration. Whatever your choice of parameter, it should be possible to get a clearer view of where competitors are currently positioned and how that is likely to change in the future by using this methodology (see Figure 7.2).

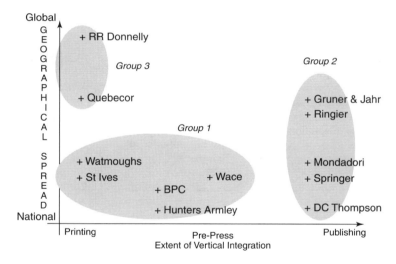

Figure 7.2   Strategic group analysis diagram

EXERCISES

Exercise 1   Five Forces Framework

Analyse the attractiveness of your industry by using the Five Forces Framework.

Enter your overall assessment of each force in the appropriate box (e.g. high–medium–low).

Threat of New Entrants

Barriers to entry:
- Economies of scale
- Distribution
- Access to raw materials
- Proprietary knowledge
- Brands

Potential retaliation from incumbents

Bargaining Power of Suppliers

Dependence on industry
Backwards integration of players
Forwards integration of suppliers
Branding/proprietary skills

Rivalry

Number and size of players
Market growth
Differentiation
High status
Diversity of interest
Exit barriers
Over capacity

Bargaining Power of Buyers

Volume purchases
Fixed costs
Backwards integration
Differentiation
Switching costs

Threat of Substitutes

Availability of close substitutes
Value to buyers
Access to capital

Exercise 2 PEST analysis

Now think back to the PEST analysis you did in Chapter 5.

How will the issues which you identified then impact on your industry and its attractiveness in the foreseeable future?

Threat of New Entrants
Barriers to entry:
- Economies of scale
- Distribution
- Access to raw materials
- Proprietary knowledge
- Brands

Potential retaliation from incumbents

Bargaining Power of Suppliers
Dependence on industry
Backwards integration of players
Forwards integration of suppliers
Branding/proprietary skills

Rivalry
Number and size of players
Market growth
Differentiation
High status
Diversity of interest
Exit barriers
Over capacity

Bargaining Power of Buyers
Volume purchases
Fixed costs
Backwards integration
Differentiation
Switching costs

Threat of Substitutes
Availability of close substitutes
Value to buyers
Access to capital

Exercise 3 Improve attractiveness of the industry

Think of ways in which you could improve the attractiveness of the industry in the future.

Exercise 4 Rivals and competitors

Now look closely at specific rivals or competitors. Analyse their strategic position by investigating the assumptions that they are operating under (e.g. 'you have to be global to survive'; 'price is the critical factor', etc.), what they are trying to achieve ('market leadership', 'consolidation', 'profitability', etc.), their strategy for achieving it ('low cost', 'superior service', 'full range', etc.) and their principal strengths and weaknesses.

	Competitor 1	*Competitor 2*	*Competitor 3*
Assumptions they make about the industry			
Objectives			
Strategy			
Strengths			
Weaknesses			

Exercise 5 Strategic group analysis

Plot your competitors according to their strategies on a chart. Using the two most important parameters as the axis (e.g. price/value v product range). Indicate with an arrow any anticipated moves.

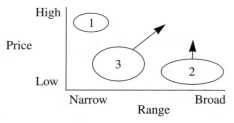

Exercise 6 What this means to your strategy

Now think: what does this analysis of competitors mean to us and to our strategy?

8 *Pulling it all together*

By now you should be much clearer as an organization about your strategic position. Before we continue into the next stage in the process, it is as well just to review and summarize where you've got to.

The thinking you have done so far may have extended over several weeks. A good idea is to hold a strategy 'retreat' to look at the company and its internal capabilities and another one some time later to look at the external trends. Now pull together the results of your analytical efforts: circulate a document in the format shown below to participants and talk the team through it at the start of the next stage. This process is useful to:

- remind busy people of views already discussed and agreed;
- demonstrate the logical flow in the process you are engaged in;
- maintain motivation by pointing out what has been achieved already;
- clarify any points at issue or add information which has emerged in the meantime.

Remember, that the process of strategic decision-making is a political process. Any changes that are subsequently made will have implications for the way power is distributed in the organization!

COMPANY NAME

Strategic Position

Internal Aspects

Mission
The company's mission is: *(insert results of Exercise 3, Chapter 1)*

Objectives
Our objectives are: *(insert results of Exercise 3, Chapter 1)*

Capabilities

Our main internal strengths are: *(insert results of Exercise 1, Chapter 2)*

From this we identified the key capabilities which can give us sustainable competitive advantage. They are: *(insert results from Exercise 2, Chapter 2)*

Some of these capabilities are fully developed; others will need to be nurtured *(insert results of Exercise 4, Chapter 2)*

Weaknesses

We also identified a number of weaknesses *(insert results of Exercise 1, Chapter 2)*

Of these only a few are critical to success and will have to be addressed or circumvented *(insert results of Exercise 4, Chapter 2)*

Logic of the Business
We reviewed the key drivers in our industry that determine success now and in the future.

CRITICAL SUCCESS FACTORS NOW   IN THE FUTURE

(insert results from Exercise 1, Chapter 3)

We compared the results of this analysis with the assumptions built into our own business about what is critical for success. We found: *(Either)*

- a high degree of fit between the way we are set up currently and the industry logic now and in the future;
- a high degree of fit with existing industry logic, but a gap between where we are currently and what is likely to be critical in the future;
- a lack of fit between our current operations and both the existing and likely future logic.

(Delete where inapplicable)

EXTERNAL ENVIRONMENT

Economic Prospects

We reviewed the prospects for the economy over the period under consideration

We made the following assumptions *(insert results from Exercise 1, Chapter 5)*

Economic growth	-	% p.a. on average
Interest rates	-	*(upper) – (lower)* %
Exchange rate	-	*(upper) – (lower)* £ against *(key currency)*

Our general view of the economy was.....................................

The impact of these assumptions on our business would be as follows:

(insert results from Exercise 1, Chapter 5)

Market size(s)   -
Market growth rate(s)   -
Margins   -

The prospects for our business are therefore ....

PEST Analysis

We analysed the business environment and identified the most important issues as.....

(insert results of Exercise 1, Chapter 6)

From our analysis it is clear that our business environment is

- static;
- relatively stable;
- starting to become less predictable;
- highly volatile and unpredictable.

(delete where inapplicable)

Industry Attractiveness

We looked at the structure of our markets and analysed how attractive our industry is now:

(insert results of Exercise 1, Chapter 7)

We reviewed this in the light of the potential changes identified in the PEST analysis and concluded that the industry was *(not)* changing

(insert results of Exercise 2, Chapter 7)

As a result, we believe that our industry is currently:

- attractive;
- unattractive.

(Delete as appropriate)

In the future, we believe our industry will be:

- more attractive;
- the same;
- less attractive.

(Delete as appropriate)

Competitor Analysis
We looked at key competitors – actual and potential – and discussed their strategies. Our analysis is summarized below:

(insert results of Exercise 4, Chapter 7)

Our expectations about competitor positioning now and in the future are depicted below:

(insert results of Exercise 5, Chapter 7)

The most important finding is.........................

Opportunities and Threats

On the basis of this review of the external environment we have identified the following:

OPPORTUNITIES   THREATS

(Fill these in based on the findings above)

9 *Creating the Right Strategy*

INTRODUCTION

Life is full of choices and for medium-sized companies getting it right could be critical. A senior executive we know put it quite well, 'We haven't got any money', she said, ' so we have to think'.

Too often we find in medium-sized businesses that options are expressed in financial terms, 'If we only we had another £500,000/£5m/£50m, what we wouldn't be able to do with this business'. When pressed to expound on this, frequently these ideas turn out to be personal hobby-horses or the products of mind-sets which have been frozen by lengthy but only partial exposure to the reality of the business.

The MD of a firm may be convinced of a need to diversify against all common sense. Top management may be married to the idea that acquiring a new piece of automated machinery will transform the company's competitive position. A new chief executive may take the company into a strategic alliance with a larger player whose success subsequently belies all the doubters.

The point is that ideas in themselves are neither intrinsically good or bad. The skill in choosing the right strategy is to be able to distinguish between robust business ideas and inappropriate personal hobby-horses. Equally, because time itself is valuable, and the outcome of strategy is important, you need to avoid the danger of 'paralysis by analysis'. How do you do that?

This chapter provides a framework through which you can:

■ think creatively about the alternative ways forward for the company;

■ reduce the available alternatives to a manageable number;

89

- evaluate the available options rigorously so that the strategy ultimately chosen achieves buy-in from the company's key stakeholders.

STRATEGIC CHOICE

In the previous chapters we looked at some of the techniques and tools that are available for analysing markets, industry structures and companies' positions within their business environment. Clearly you need to think about where you are and what is happening to your world before you can make any decisions about where you go forward. And, having done that analysis, it is important to move from that to actually selecting the proper course of action. This section will then look at a systematic way for generating the various options which are open to companies.

The point about choosing a strategy is that there should be a fit between a firm's core competences, and the way that its environment is developing. If you like, there must be a match between the strengths and weaknesses and the opportunities and threats.

Of course, it is always possible to sit down and brainstorm for yourself, from your analysis of the company and its situation, a number of different courses of action. This has the advantage that your alternatives will be tailored to your own particular situation; it has the disadvantage that you might miss out on a possible option which you may not have thought of, but which may well be available to you. There are a number of simple models which have been developed, tried and tested over the last few decades, and have proved their worth repeatedly in business situations. Figure 9.1 shows a diagram of the various strategic alternatives open to a company.

The model distinguishes between three types of strategies: *generic strategies*, which are how a company competes within its chosen industry, *alternative directions* which are about choosing from amongst various options for growth, and *alternative methods* which are about how you actually implement those alternative directions. More simply then the strategies boil down to:

- What basis are we going to compete on?
- Which direction are we heading?
- How are we getting there?

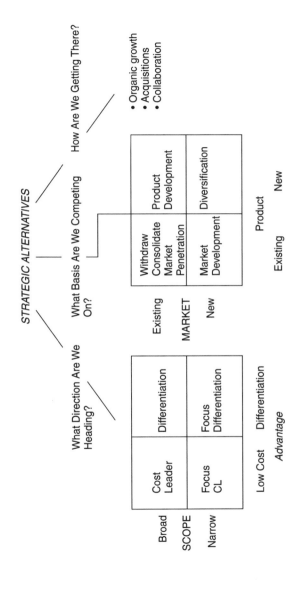

Figure 9.1 Strategic Alternatives (Based on: G Johnson and K Scholes, *Exploring Corporate Strategy* (Prentice Hall 1993) and on the work of Michael Porter and Igor Ansoff)

Competitive Strategies

We will look first at choosing strategies which will provide the firm with a sustainable source of competitive advantage. Michael Porter, who first developed these strategies, referred to them as generic strategies because he believed that no matter what industry or market a company was in it had to make certain fundamental choices about how it should compete. Essentially, a company can compete either on the basis of cost leadership or on the basis of differentiation. It could do this either across the industry, by offering a product or a service in each segment, or by focusing in more narrowly and competing in a particular market segment, a stage of the value chain or a geographical area. Hence there are four basic positions.

To be a successful *cost leader* implies that you will produce goods or services at the lowest possible costs, or at least lower than any other competitor in your industry. In theory there should be only one cost leader in any industry. Unsuccessful cost leaders should be driven out of business as successful cost leaders are able to undercut them and expand their market share. In practice, however, due for instance to government interventions such as subsidies, or due to different sources of cost advantage – for example, automation versus low-cost sourcing of components – there is often more than one company in any industry competing on the basis of cost. In electricity generation, for instance, both National Power and Powergen seek to be the cost leaders in their industry.

To be a successful *differentiator* implies that you must produce goods or services which in some way have unique characteristics which the customer is willing to pay for. So whilst cost leaders make their money by producing at a lower cost than anybody else, differentiators will make their money from selling at a premium. As already mentioned, you can compete on a broad basis or focus in on a narrower target and compete either on the basis of cost or differentiation.

You may find this concept of generic strategies rather strange at first. A good way of understanding it more fully is to try to apply it to a well known industry. Take the example of the UK supermarket industry. Can you think of any examples of companies that are pursuing differentiation strategies-i.e. they are trying to compete across the board and are offering certain benefits to consumers for which consumers are willing to pay a bit extra, over and above the standard product being offered in the market place?

Good examples of differentiators in this industry would be Waitrose, Tesco or Sainsbury's. What about companies pursuing a cost leadership strategy? Well, a clear example here is Kwiksave. Interestingly, Kwiksave seems to have filled the gap in the market as Tesco (the original 'pile 'em high and sell 'em cheap' company!) migrated to become a differentiator.

How easy is it for a company to shift its position from one generic strategy to another? Clearly it is possible, as the example of Tesco shows, and in some situations it may be necessary. In Tesco's case, for example, the switch of strategies was clearly underpinned by the assessment of where the market was going in the 1980s, i.e. the consumers would be willing to spend more for a wider variety of food sold in more convenient and commodious surroundings. This differentiation strategy does not exclude the use of price as a marketing weapon. However, for Tesco or Sainsbury's to suddenly compete now on the basis of price as a long-term competitive strategy would not be sustainable. Why would this be the case?

If you think about it, the differentiation strategies of Tesco and Sainsbury's are based on long-term investments in out-of-town sites, large purpose-built stores containing a wide range of different goods, including fresh food, well spaced out with wide aisles and serviced by relatively well-trained personnel. The overhead costs of investment in these sites and the costs of maintaining this differentiation edge would make it difficult for Sainsbury's or Tesco to compete on the basis of price with the true cost leaders. For example, in order to achieve its cost leadership position Kwiksave has largely ignored out-of-town sites and chosen to locate in relatively small premises within towns. The space within the stores is usually limited, as is the product range which is normally displayed in cardboard boxes. Personnel support is strictly limited and employment costs kept to a minimum.

Clearly Kwiksave has organized itself around its competitive strategy of pursuing cost-leadership. This would make it difficult for the broadly based differentiators to launch a major attack against it on the basis of price. Cost leaders, however, are always vulnerable to new entrants and other players reinventing themselves and redesigning their value chains to lower the costs still further. So Kwiksave is threatened, for example, by the German chain Aldi and the Danish chain Netto, who have entered the market on the back of the opportunities offered by the Single European Market. They in turn are now being challenged by the US Warehouse Clubs who have reinvented retailing to drive costs down even further. So, being a cost leader and sustaining that position requires a great deal of ingenuity and constant search for efficiency improvements.

What about the focused differentiators? Good examples of companies pursuing this strategy in the supermarket industry would be Marks and Spencer in their food department, or, even more focused and differentiated, Fortnum and Mason and Harrods. Differentiators face their own risks, however. Can you think what they might be?

Well, one of the main risks of differentiation is that the source of your differentiation becomes eroded over time. Companies that differentiate themselves on the basis of quality, for example, may find it difficult to sustain that position when the other competitors in the market-place have reached the same standard of quality. Another major problem associated with differentiation is the cost of achieving it. A lot of German companies in the 1990s, for example, thought that their technological excellence and reputation for quality would isolate them from price competition. However, with the structural rigidities in the German economy, particularly the high costs of labour, their costs had reached a position where they wiped out most of the advantage accruing from being able to charge a premium for their products. Even well-established companies with strong brand names like BMW, Mercedes and Volkswagen faced this problem.

Are these generic strategies mutually exclusive or should companies pursue them in parallel? Porter, who originated this framework, would argue that you *must* choose definitely what your source of competitive advantage is and how you are going to compete. Failing to make this decision, i.e. by trying to compete on both cost leadership *and* on differentiation, would in his view probably lead to a company being 'stuck in the middle' and as a result performing less well than companies pursuing pure cost leadership or differentiation strategies.

The research on this is not conclusive. There is some evidence that companies *can* successfully combine the pursuit of cost leadership and the ability to differentiate. This may happen, for example, through the adoption of 'lean' production technology which allows companies to be both more responsive to the market place and to reduce costs. In fact, to give him his due, Porter does *not* argue that cost leaders should ignore differentiation or that differentiators should be oblivious to costs. Rather, his position is that differentiators should reduce costs in all aspects of their business up to, but not beyond, the point at which it starts to damage their differentiation edge. Likewise, cost leaders should try to differentiate their products, but only to the point at which it damages their cost position *vis à vis* their competitors.

The most recent research would seem to indicate that superior returns can be achieved by companies which successfully pursue both cost leadership and differentiation and such companies will outperform pure cost leaders or pure differentiators. However, it is also the most difficult trick to pull off. Our own view is that there is some virtue in selecting one or another of the generic strategies as the main thrust because the organizational implications of going for one rather than the other may be quite profound as the comparison between Kwiksave and Tesco would demonstrate. There are, in fact, a number of companies in the supermarket industry which tried to pursue both (or neither!) and came to grief as a result. Asda (in the past) and Gateway could be classed as 'stuck in the middle' companies, for instance. In practice, almost equally problematic for companies, particularly medium-sized companies, is to be stuck in the middle between being broadly based and narrowly focused. This is a problem in industries where economies of scale are important and where medium-sized companies end up being not large enough to compete on the basis of costs with more broadly based competitors, yet too broadly based to specialize on a particular niche. Fokker in aircraft and Rover in cars both exemplify this problem.

What generic strategies, therefore, are likely to be more appropriate for medium-sized companies? In general small and medium-sized companies, in order to sustain their competitive positions, would be well advised to focus on a narrower scope than larger companies. This enables them to concentrate their resources and not dissipate their strength. Whether to compete on cost or whether to compete on differentiation depends on the nature of the industry and also on the skills and competences of the company concerned. Cost-based strategies are likely to be most successful in segments which are not volume sensitive and do not require high investment in plant or products to deliver low cost. It is perfectly possible for medium-sized companies to compete with larger players on cost if larger competitors are carrying high overheads from their total business. Small car hire companies, for example, compete against industry giants like Hertz and Avis. Large competitors may have the advantage of being able to cross-subsidize or assault the smaller player's market place, however.

Many successful medium-sized firms dominate quite small niches through sustained technological innovation. This is sustainable if the niche is large enough and does not decline due to technological obsolencence or if the niche is not so attractive that it outstrips the company's ability to invest and remain competitive.

Alternative Directions

In the introduction we looked at the business of defining the company's mission and objectives. It is common for companies as part of that process to set targets for both return on investment and growth. The strategy chosen should then indicate how those targets are going to be met. One way of exploring the options is to sketch the alternatives on the Ansoff matrix in Exercise 2 at the end of the chapter.

This model, named after one of the most influential writers on strategy since the 1960s, sets out the alternative directions open to a company. If you were applying the model, which quadrant do you think you would start at first? Well, most people would start at the top left with the most familiar, exploring the options for existing products in existing markets. A number of options are outlined in the quadrant. To do nothing is generally not a credible strategy, particularly in the face of a changing market place. Withdrawal and/or liquidation may well be a suitable option. If the company is not interested in a particular business because it does not fit within its overall strategic intent, it does not maximize any of its existing strengths or does not provide any other benefits, e.g. good short term returns, withdrawing maybe the best solution. This will enable the company to refocus its attention and concentrate its resources on other more viable businesses. Likewise, consolidation of the business, for example by restructuring it to lower its cost position, may be a vital condition of survival in the market place and/or a way of stemming a haemorrhage of cash.

To grow in this position, however, requires *market penetration*. This means, in effect that you are increasing your market share of your existing markets by using your existing products. Market penetration *may* be a highly advantageous option. For example, in a declining market it could enable a company to soak up the remaining demand in the market place and ensure the continuation of distribution channels. Similarly, in volume sensitive industries where costs decline as volume increases a policy of market penetration can be a vital underpinning for a successful cost leadership strategy.

Assume that the company has explored the options for market penetration but has concluded that this is not really appropriate. It may be that the market is saturated and that the costs of growing in this market through expanding its market share may just be too much. Alternatively, and this happens particularly with the privatized utilities in the UK, there could be regulatory reasons why the company may not be allowed to increase its market share. In other words, it may be contravening legislation on monopolies. So, what other options exist for a company? Well a company could try to grow through exploring new markets with its existing products, in effect, pursuing *market development*. Alternatively a company could stay in its existing markets but develop new products. We call this *product development*.

Which option do you think companies should pursue first, market development or product development?

As you probably guessed the answer depends very much on what type of business you are in. For example, classically a lot of companies in capital intensive industries have used market development strategies first. Usually they have invested in plant and equipment for the domestic market. But in order to utilize it more effectively they have looked around for other markets On the other hand, if you are in a business which is characterized by short product life cycles where, in order to stay ahead, you have to be launching new products regularly, then product development may well be the most effective strategic approach to take.

Assume that you have looked at these two options and concluded that market development is not suitable, because foreign competitors have got the other markets sewn up or foreign governments are blocking market entry. Assume also that product development is not suitable because the market is conservative or your company has no skills in house in developing new products. What is the remaining option open to the company?

The last avenue is diversification, which means trying to grow in new markets with new products. Diversification is often said to be the most risky of the options available to the company, because you are compounding your risk by entering a new market with a new product. That is why Ansoff proposed that a company should first explore the other options before looking at diversification.

In fact, there is quite a lot of research available to us now which reinforces the view that diversification – in particular unrelated diversification, where companies enter into completely different markets with totally unrelated technologies or products – has a high risk of failure. This is not to say that diversification *per se* is a bad thing. A lot of companies in the defence industry, for example, have had to diversify into civilian markets since the late eighties with the collapse in defence spending due to the end of the Cold War. Some, but by no means all, have been successful. Companies diversify for a number of legitimate reasons:

- existing markets may be saturated or in decline;
- their existing markets may be limited by regulatory controls;
- they may feel that being focused on one particular business exposes them to a downturn in the market, and diversification is therefore seen as a way of balancing that risk.

Alas, too often in business, diversification is the result of ill thought-out actions. Businesses in unrelated areas are acquired, because they are available and the price seems attractive. Only subsequently is any thought given to how they will be integrated within the overall strategy. A new market is entered on the strength of expertise in another market, without thinking through the additional requirements that are going to be needed to make a success of the new market, which may require very different distribution channels, pricing and promotional activities. Similarly, often little thought is given to how diversification should be managed. If diversification is going to be a key part of the business strategy, and not simply a financial investment in another business which can be managed as a portfolio investment on an arm's length basis, then it will have to be integrated within the company's strategy and managed so as to achieve the maximum benefit for the company as a whole. Management time will have to be devoted to executing a successful diversification. Reporting structures, management teams, career patterns and working practices will all have to be adjusted accordingly.

In general it is safer, particularly for small to medium-sized companies, to focus on the business they know about rather than trying to expand in every direction. Diversification should, wherever possible, be limited to related diversification.

This may mean branching out horizontally. Makers of electronic personal organizers like Psion, for example, are looking to diversify into mobile phones as they perceive that the two markets are converging. This may also involve moving up or down the value chain.

You could integrate *backwards* – e.g. a manufacturer of electric motors moves back down the chain to make some of the components – or *forward* – e.g. a manufacturer decides to move into wholesale distribution. These are known as 'make or buy' decisions and they are one of the most important sets of strategic decisions a company has to make. In effect, the question is 'Which stages of the value chain does the company have to own and control itself, and which can be sub-contracted to other players?'

In the past, companies, particularly manufacturing companies, have often owned and controlled as much of the value chain as possible. Sometimes, particularly with owner-managed companies, this has been driven by the top leader's paranoia – Ford and Unilever are good examples. In other cases vertical integration has been seen as a way of keeping out new entrants from the market. These days companies are having to look much more closely at their position along the value chain. The general rule of thumb is that companies should stick to those aspects of their operations where they have some kind of competitive advantage, where they can do it better or more cheaply than other players in the industry. So, a company may be a good designer and assembler, for example, but would not necessarily have to make all the parts. Where a company does not have a competitive advantage, it should consider sub-contracting or 'out-sourcing'. In theory, at least, this should allow maximum gains from specialization to occur. As always, there are no hard and fast rules, however. The UK's most successful company in value creation terms is DFS, an integrated manufacturer and retailer of furniture.

Unrelated diversification, as has already been mentioned, carries a high risk of failure and should be entered into with caution. There may be some occasions, however, where unrelated diversification is appropriate, at least temporarily. We came across a company in Russia recently that was highly diversified for such a small organization. Its core business was in the manufacture of trailers for cars, but it also produced marble cladding for walls, toys, holiday tours and medical instruments. Naturally we asked the managing director what the common thread was that united all the various parts of his business. He replied candidly that there was no particular business thread but that in the conditions currently prevailing in the Russian market place nobody knew who the players would be tomorrow or what markets would continue to exist or grow. He knew that not all of his businesses would survive and thrive but until a degree of stability was restored he was determined to keep as many irons in the fire as possible!

Alternative Methods

You have now looked at how you are going to compete and grow. Now you need to decide how you are going to get there. If the market is growing strongly and the company has the resources, both human and financial to support growth, *organic* or internal development may be feasible. For example, a number of companies in the computer industry have risen from nothing to being major league competitors in the space of a few years. Dell computers in hardware, for example, and Microsoft in software are good examples of companies which have grown, essentially through internal development on the back of a sustainable competitive advantage. Some companies and cultures prefer to grow in any case through internal development because they find it easier to manage the process of growth through simply replicating their existing systems rather than trying to absorb an alien culture or approach. Thus many Japanese companies prefer to work with green-field sites.

If speed is important or if the industry is restructuring as a result of a move towards maturity, for example, then growth by internal development is likely to be less appropriate than acquisitions, mergers or collaboration. Acquisitions can enable a company to consolidate its position in an industry thus both strengthening its competitive position and improving the average profitability for the industry as a whole by creating fewer larger players. Acquisitions can enable companies to fill a gap in their product range, to gain access to new skills or technology, or to gain access to new markets and market segments. BMW's acquisition of Rover, for example, achieved all three of these.

However, as with diversification, acquisitions should be treated with a great deal of caution. The research reveals again and again the risks entailed in carrying out acquisitions. By any standard, only half of the acquisitions which are carried out are subsequently deemed to be successful. Fifty per cent fail to meet their goals and indeed it is a revealing finding of the research on acquisitions that the prime beneficiary of acquisitions seems to be the shareholders – of the company that is being acquired! In other words, very often companies overestimate both the latent potential of their acquisition target, as well as the potential benefits of merging it with their own organization and end up paying too much for the acquisition. For medium-sized companies acquisitions can be high risk as they will typically constitute a significant part of the business which, if things turn sour, could prove life-threatening

One way to avoid the risks of acquisition is to pursue a strategy of joint development or collaboration. This involves linking up with another company. For medium-sized companies this often means linking up with a larger company. The relationship could take a number of forms:

- co-marketing deals where the companies agree to market each others' products;
- licensing to a larger company with a more developed sales force a product developed by the smaller company;
- collaboration on joint research products;
- common manufacturing facilities;
- ultimately, a full blown merger.

Joint development may be a particularly attractive method for smaller businesses which do not have the necessary funds to develop new products or to commercialize or to distribute them. Excellent companies like Unipart, the car component maker, have benefited from long-term relationships with larger manufacturers. By securing business relations with industry leaders quality and productivity can be raised to new standards. In return medium-sized companies can aspire to be first or second tier suppliers to manufacturer assemblers, taking responsibility for the design and production or sub-assemblies or components.

However, companies need to be aware of some of the pitfalls involved in managing collaborative arrangements. First, if the collaboration involves working together (as opposed to simply licensing technology or swapping products) then the likelihood is that it will be more successful if it has its own management structure, its own defined targets and responsibilities and its own loyalties and incentives. Second, companies, particularly small and medium-sized companies, should go into alliances with open eyes. People and companies enter joint ventures because they do not possess a particular resource or capability. Astute companies use joint ventures as a way of acquiring those capabilities. Japanese companies, in particular, are past masters at this. Joint ventures in effect are a race to learn: a partner who adopts a learning mode and absorbs as quickly as possible the part of the business which its partner currently possesses, will ultimately end up with the dominant position within the joint venture. Joint ventures, can last a long time – the Fujitsu-Xerox combination has operated successfully since the 1960s. Often, however, the result is that either one or other of the partners acquires a majority stake or there is a break-up of the partnership.

CREATING NEW STRATEGIES

So far, our approach has been rather analytical. It is fine to be systematic and thought through, but where is the spark in your thinking that will differentiate you from other competitors? New ideas can suggest:

- novel ways of sustaining a cost leadership strategy by re-configuring key processes;
- ways in which you can differentiate your products and services with new features;
- methods of locking customers in for the long term;
- applications in other sectors for technology you have developed.

The techniques of strategy are widely available and understood by many firms. They are certainly accessible to your competitors and they may indeed be using the same principles and models as you are! How can you add to the models something which is unique and which appeals to customers in a way that makes other products and services look run of the mill? Many of the most successful companies in recent years have achieved their position by upsetting received wisdom: Direct Line insurance and Daewoo in cars show the value of creativity.

For many of us, an intimate knowledge of the business in which we operate is our biggest asset. We like to think we understand our customers, what they need and what they might want in the future. We understand the technology involved in the business – what is possible and profitable and what is not. We also know the main competitors in the market, what they can do and what their aspirations are.

But the line between experience and habit is a fine one. While experience of a business can guide our strategies, it might also make us cling to old assumptions long after they are in any way helpful. We can find ourselves stuck in unprofitable ruts, while the rest of the market, our competitors and new players have moved on. This was a problem which affected Arjo Wiggins, the paper maker. A market leader in paper with its 'Conqueror' brand, it failed to spot a shift in end user behaviour.

In looking for arresting new options, we need to be creative in our thinking at each stage of the strategy process. We need to use techniques and approaches which help us shift our thinking. Creativity techniques can help us to see old problems in a new light and think 'outside the box'.

One good approach is to use analogous thinking, that is we identify a problem or an issue in our business and try to find an analogy or a metaphor from another area of activity. Then we take the solutions worked through in the world of the analogy and try to transfer them to the real world. If you have been able to let go of the real world and work through possible solutions in the imagined world of the analogy, you may come up with solutions to your original question that you would never have thought of and that may surprise you at their novelty and their potential usefulness. For example, a company which faced an intractable crisis drew on the expression 'up a creek without a paddle' as a succinct description of its position! It then identified within the analogy the possible solutions: using other implements, going with the flow, abandoning ship, draining the creek, etc. Finally, it looked at how these ideas could be translated back into the original organizational setting: finding alternative sources of funding, restructuring to be more responsive, going bankrupt etc.

Of course, you may encounter problems in using creative thinking techniques. One is a feeling of discomfort that might prompt you to go for safe territory. So, for example, when using analogous thinking we might choose an example which we know is not very far away from the real world problem and/or use examples in the analogy which provide solutions that are already well known in the real world. If we do that, then it is not surprising that we may come up with solutions that work. But we could have worked it out without using the technique.

Inevitably, creativity training takes time. You need to get used to the feeling of working in free-thinking mode. As you become more familiar with the approach and more comfortable with working in that way, you can push yourself harder. So, for example, if you used analogous thinking as an approach, you might decide to outlaw analogies that use football or other sporting teams – they are too close to our experience and outcomes will often be too predictable. Instead use an analogy that at first does *not* seem to be a good metaphor for your problem. You will have to think hard to get into the parallel and work through solutions that seem only applicable to that area of activity and not at all related to the original question. This is not a waste of time: many major advances in science owe their discovery, not so much to a continuation of research in that particular field, but to insights developed in other quite unrelated areas of science. Ways of answering questions – or indeed ways of posing them – that have proved useful in one area can be transferred to another to advantage. Advances in artifical limbs for example benefited from insights derived from shock absorber technology.

Another useful exercise involves using a list of words as a trigger to your thinking. Start off by choosing at random a list of five words that are related to the original question. Say, for example, a group of people working in this mode are considering the problem of how to develop a new product line in an existing market. That product might be chocolate bars. They select ten words related to chocolate bars. They then narrow down their selection to the five words which most appeal to them. The challenge then is to work out solutions, related to each one of these five words. Like analogous thinking, the usefulness of this technique is that it acts as a catalyst to explore 'uncharted' area, to see things in new ways and to bring together previously unrelated ideas in a form which makes sense.

As you gain familiarity with creative approaches try using five unrelated words to start the process. The more we have to stretch our minds to think of solutions from this starting point, the more likely we are to move ourselves out of our rut and create options for our business which have not been thought of by other companies, even though they might be using the same models, operating in the same markets, or experiencing the same pressures.

At the outset it is important to establish a few ground rules for creative thinking The most important rule is not to condemn, at too early a stage, ideas that seem crazy. By definition, some of the greatest ideas will initially seem 'off the wall' or out of line with conventional wisdom. At this stage, being over evaluative or critical can kill good ideas.

The second ground rule is to build on the ideas of others. Common practice in business is to serve to demonstrate how good *your* idea is in comparison with others. Frequently, our organizational cultures encourage competitive individualistic behaviour. Creative thinking requires a supportive approach. Try to draw in people and build on their ideas. Savour the delight of finding an idea, receiving it when it has been passed on by someone else, exploring and expanding it then passing it on to someone else to grow it!

EVALUATING STRATEGIC OPTIONS

Strategic thinking involves a range of different modes of thinking. At times, we need to be analytical and rational. And whilst, as we have seen, we need to be open minded and creative, even the most imaginative ideas have to be subjected to the hard test of reality. We suggest here a simple way that you can rigorously evaluate the various options you have created (see Table 9.1).

The first criterion that we use is *suitability*. Remember we said that strategy is often thought of as trying to achieve a match between the circumstances in which a company finds itself, its strengths and its weaknesses, and the possibilities open to it, the opportunities and the threats? Well suitability is about achieving this fit. Go back to the diagram of the various options open to us (Figure 9.1).

The first set of choices we had to make was how we are going to compete. Cost leadership may be a suitable strategy to pursue if the organization is capable of being structured for production efficiency, if it is large enough to benefit from the economies of scale and if the market place is sensitive to price. Small and medium-sized companies, in particular, have to be realistic. Industry giants can prove to have feet of clay: many small computer companies, for

Table 9.1   Criteria for Evaluating Strategic Options

CRITERIA	MEANING
SUITABILITY	Does the option fit the firm's situation? Is there evidence from research to support it?
FEASIBILITY	Have we got the resources to do it? Likely competitor response?
ACCEPTABILITY	Is it consistent with our mission? Does it meet our objectives? Will our stakeholders approve? Is the risk containable?

Based on: G. Johnson and K. Scholes, *Exploring Corporate Strategy*, (Prentice Hall 1993)

example, gained at the expense of IBM in the early 1990s. But, in classic manufacturing industries, a dominant market player like Boeing, say, in aircraft manufacturing, can enjoy unassailable advantages over small challengers. You don't 'tug on Superman's cape' and it would be unwise to attempt a full frontal assault on a major industry player like Boeing. Smaller companies that seek to compete on cost leadership would probably be well advised to focus on a narrower market scope. Often it is possible to focus on niches which are not profitable for large companies or which cannot be exploited by industry giants because of their cost structure. Low overheads, low asset intensity (e.g. through leasing equipment) networking with other players or exploiting spot markets can make focus cost leadership an attractive option. Easyjet is the latest company to spot opportunites in the liberalizing airline markets of Europe to undercut less efficient airlines.

Turn to alternative directions. A lot of companies that start off in relatively small geographical markets – firms in some of the smaller European companies and the Scandinavian countries for example – soon feel the limitations of focusing on their home market. Very often they pursue market development strategies. Similarly, companies that are in very volatile or cyclical industries – up one minute and down the next – often find it prudent to have a second leg which is more stable and less sensitive to variations in overall economic activity. A lot of the accounting firms, for example, will have both consulting activity, which is lucrative but cyclical, as well as the more mundane but stable revenue which they generate from auditing activities.

Finally, consider the alternative methods. Acquisitions are likely to be most suitable when markets are maturing and industry structure is shaking out. As demand declines so the industry will likely support fewer players. At this point, very often the major players will seek to consolidate their position through acquisitions. Alternatively, acquisitions can be used to enter new markets. Acquisitions may be preferred in such situations over forming joint ventures because of the greater control which integrating activities within the company gives. Acquisitions also enable companies to enter new markets or offer new products without years of delay.

How can we know more about what options are likely to be most suitable for us in our situation? Well, in Chapter 4 we looked at the sort of strategies that seemed to be successful for small and medium-sized enterprises. Clearly, the type of strategy you adopt will depend on the stage the industry is at, whether it is embryonic, growing, mature or declining. In Table 9.2 we suggest some of the more appropriate strategies for these different phases, and in the references at the back of the book we give you some further sources to look for if you are interested in any of those particular stages of development.

Let us assume that you have already identified the options and screened them for suitability. Assume three options have some strategic logic given the situation that you are in:

- complete withdrawal from this industry and refocusing of efforts on to a different business area;
- refocusing on one particular segment where you have a competitive advantage; disposal of all activities outside this segment; competing within this segment on the basis of differentiated goods and services;
- continuing to operate as a broadly-based differentiator in the same market segments but seeking a partner to strengthen your position with a view to consolidating industry structure.

These three options are all suitable given the circumstances. Now you need to evaluate them in terms of their *feasibility* and their *acceptability*. Acceptability is the extent to which an option meets

Table 9.2   Strategies for Industry Stages

INDUSTRY GROWTH PHASE	STRATEGIC CHOICES
EMBRYONIC	▪ Establish the market need for the product or service. Grow the market ▪ Encourage competitors to enter to provide assurance for customers ▪ Cultivate lead customers to demonstrate the product value ▪ Look for the breakthrough innovation which will trigger exponential growth
GROWTH	▪ Invest heavily to dominate the market/format. Reinvest profits: Grow with the market, avoid market share battles ▪ Profit from superior power/information as a supplier *vis à vis* buyers to make short-term profits without entering into long-term commitments
MATURITY	▪ Maintain market leadership. Invest in efficiency and/or differentiation ▪ Grow through acquisition to become industry leader ▪ Reconfigure the industry's value chain ▪ Focus on a particular niche or segment or stage in the value chain ▪ Withdraw/re-invent the business
DECLINE	▪ maintain or increase market share (by acquisition) if the industry is profitable and the firm's position is strong ▪ Shrink selectively by exiting from weak positions ▪ Harvest existing business by profit taking with the intention ultimately of withdrawal ▪ Immediate withdrawal or closure

the objectives that were set at the start of the process and is consistent with the overall mission of the company. It would also have to be acceptable to the company's major stakeholders, institutional investors, for example, or its work-force. Total withdrawal, for example, may well be a *suitable* strategy given the opportunity costs involved, but if your mission statement defined this as the business that you should be in, then why should you contemplate, at least in the first instance, withdrawal from the industry? Focusing on a particular niche may prove to be a more defensible strategy: it will enable you to sustain your competitive position and remain within the industry, albeit as a minor player. On the other hand, the sort of downsizing entailed by this strategy may well be opposed by the employees in the company. The third strategic option will certainly meet your mission and your objectives, and is likely to be acceptable to most of your stakeholders, although there may be some objections to you merging your identity with another company, particularly if there is some relocation of resources.

But which of the three alternatives is likely to be the most feasible? Which will promise you the best returns? Which has the best combination of risk to benefit? On the face of it, at least, the third option would seem to involve the most risk. Mergers and acquisitions, after all, are notorious for going wrong. Nevertheless, you should also not ignore the risk of becoming ghettoized within a shrinking segment in the market place or of retreating in the face of competition into an unsustainable niche. As far as returns are concerned, clearly the second option will involve a reduction in overall turnover, but not necessarily in the returns that you make on the sales that you do achieve. This would depend on a number of things: your cost position and the logic of operating in this particular industry: for example, how important are economies of scale?

Ultimately, these questions can only be *definitively* answered, if at all, in retrospect. However, that is really not good enough from your point of view: the end point in this process must be a decision on which strategy is the best one to pursue. In the examples that we have given we would probably eliminate the first option as being inconsistent with the company's basic mission. Choosing between the second and third option would involve further discussion and evaluation since the implications of the options are quite profound for the future of the company.

Evaluating Strategic Options – an example

The management team of a UK manufacturer conducted a full strategic review. After eliminating some options – diversification because of constraints imposed by group headquarters for instance – they consolidated the list of options into six:

1 *Harvest.* This meant taking out profits and only investing enough in the business to keep it going and prevent a decline in efficiency. This would result in a gradual erosion of competitive position and market share and ultimately greatly reduced profits.

2 *Harvest except for investment in new finishing equipment.* This would slow the rate of decline by improving efficiency (several jobs would be eliminated) and enhancing the quality of the end product. The basic process would remain the same and a loss of competitive position could not be helped in the long term.

3 *Invest in a completely new green-field site.* As an alternative to developing the existing works this would involve investing in a completely new plant in a favourable location, installing automated state-of-the-art machinery and introducing flexible working practices from scratch. This would involve a doubling of existing capacity and a run down of the old works.

4 *Re-equip the existing site.* This would entail installing state-of-the-art machinery, allowing the company to compete for larger sales, generating cost savings from long production runs, stealing a march on UK competition and penetrating European markets.

5 *Acquire a European competitor.* A substantial investment which could only be made with the consent of the target, which assumes that the target company is in need of support to bolster its competitive position. This would involve acquiring a factory with modern plant and increasing production capacity all in one go. It could provide greater manufacturing flexibility, access to continental markets and greater production security for customers.

6 *Re-equip the existing plant step by step.* Stagger the investment decisions over time and tailor investment to emerging market trends. Close down old machinery to maintain existing overall capacity levels at lower operating costs.

The management team devised their own set of criteria to evaluate the option (Table 9.3)

On the basis of the evaluation they opted for Option 4.

Table 9.3   Strategic Option Criteria Matrix

		1	2	3	4	5	6
A	Does it meet our objectives?	No	No	Yes	Yes	Emphasis on Growth	Partially
B	Does it fit with state of the industry/trends in external environment?	No	Partially	Yes	Yes	No	Yes
C	Does it capitalize on our core competences?	No	No	Yes	Yes	Yes	Yes
D	Does it involve major upheaval and cultural change?	No	No	Yes - but manageable	Yes - but integrated into the strategy	No	Yes - but integrated into the strategy
E	Do we have/can we obtain, the resources to do it?	Yes	Yes	Yes	Yes	Possibly	Yes
F	What are the risks of failure? Are they commensurate with the benefits?	Low	Low	High	Medium	High	Medium
G	Will it give us a sustainable competitive advantage?	No	No	Yes	Yes	No	No

As we did the exercise it became clear that option 4 was the best choice. We might have got there eventually in any case, but the discipline of thinking through the options systematically was useful, not least because it surfaced a lot of options and gut feelings which we were able to take apart (relatively) dispassionately. It also enabled us to build a case for a forward looking strategy to take to 'corporate' who, in turn, had to satisfy the City that we had our act together.

EXERCISES

Exercise 1 Porter's strategy matrix and your company

Consider the four basic positions on Porter's generic strategy matrix. Indicate how, if at all, each strategy could be adapted to your company. For example:

Example:

COMPETITIVE
SCOPE

Broad

Narrow

	CL - not possible given size and market share	**DIFF.** - need alliance or partnership to cover market
	FOCUS CL - possible through outsourcing, leasing producing in assisted area, automated assembly	**FOCUS DIFF.** - possible by tailoring product or service, establishing reputation

Cost Leadership   Differentiation
COMPETITIVE ADVANTAGE

Now complete the grid:

	CL	DIFF.
Broad		
COMPETITIVE SCOPE	**FOCUS CL**	**FOCUS DIFF.**
Narrow		

Cost Leadership   Differentiation
COMPETITIVE ADVANTAGE

Exercise 2 The Ansoff matrix and your company

Consider the four directions on the Ansoff matrix below. Indicate how, if at all, each direction might apply to your firm:
Example:

PRODUCTS

	Existing	New
Existing	**Market Penetration Withdrawal** Consolidation - some growth possible if quality improves	**Product Development** - adaptation of existing products - spin-offs
New	**Market Development** - overseas development - franchising	**Diversification** - horizontal too risky - limited forward integration, e.g. factory shops

MARKETS

Now complete the grid:

	Existing	**PRODUCTS**	New

<table>
<tr><td rowspan="2" align="right">Existing</td><td></td><td></td></tr>
<tr><td></td><td></td></tr>
<tr><td align="right">MARKETS</td><td></td><td></td></tr>
<tr><td align="right">New</td><td></td><td></td></tr>
</table>

Exercise 3 Alternative strategy methods

Consider the alternative strategy methods below. Indicate how each might be adapted to your firm.

Example:

METHOD	APPLICATION
Organic	Establishing branch network Setting up overseas subsidiary
Collaborative	Franchising: licensing technology joint venture overseas
Acquisition	Merging with large firm: acquiring a competitor; buying a supplier

Now complete the grid:

METHOD	APPLICATION
Organic	
Collaborative	
Acquisition	

Exercise 4 Creative Thinking

1 By brainstorming think of a colourful analogy of your firm's position.

2 Staying in the analogy try to generate as many alternative ways of addressing the situation as possible.

3 Now return to your firm's strategic position. How could you translate the solutions you came up with in the analogy into the real world?

4 Review the results. Enter any good ideas in the grids in Exercises 1 – 3 or make a separate note.

Exercise 5 Evaluating Options

1 Eliminate all the options which are not suitable given your analysis of your strengths and weaknesses and the opportunities and threats. Focus on those options which build on the firm's capabilities and offer the prospect of sustainable competitive advantage.

2 Eliminate all options which are not feasible from a resource point of view; which would entail too great a risk or might provoke a fierce competitor reaction.

3 Eliminate all options which will not fulfil the firm's objectives or be consistent with its mission.

4 Select from those options which are suitable, feasible and acceptable the best combination to:

(a) build a sound long term competitive position;

(b) provide good returns;

(c) satisfy key stakeholders.

10 *Enacting Strategy*

INTRODUCTION

So far in this book we have provided a rigorous and creative approach to thinking about strategy. You have seen the research evidence which explains what makes small and medium-sized enterprises successful. You have gone through a process which has related change in the external environment to internal core competencies and capabilities of your organization and you have begun to develop a strategy.

You have thought strategically. But strategy is not simply about planning, the outcome of this strategic process will be action and change. You now need to plan in order to make these actions and change actually happen.

Throughout the book you have come across a number of paradoxes that you encounter in your business, such as:

- The need to ensure 'buy-in' and commitment from people in the business, while at the same time providing direction and leadership.
- The need to understand intimately the market and the environment, while at the same time recognizing that change and volatility renders experience less relevant.
- The need to ensure involvement and understanding of the process, while at the same time being able to think objectively.
- The need to encourage flexibility of thought and of actions and flexibility in any plans, while at the same time needing to create a clear intent as you go forward in your business.

So how do you go about enacting the strategy? Two things are clear: one, it is a messy process which is rarely sequential. It is not a matter of designing a strategy and then using textbook project management techniques to launch it. Indeed, the very design of this book has reflected this complicated process. From the beginning we suggested you work through this book not on your own and not just with your management team, but also with a range of people throughout your organization. The reason is that even the development of strategy itself is part of its implementation. The second point that is clear is that there is no one, single, best, solution to developing and enacting a strategy. Think back to the beginning of this book when you reflected on your planning style. You will recall that the selection of an appropriate planning style was conditioned by a number of factors both internal and external to the organization. These included your company or national culture, the kind of business that you are in – whether it is opportunistic and short term in its focus or one which is much prone to planning for the long term – and the preferences of the people in your organization.

Just as your planning style depends on different factors and will be shaped by them, so, too, the approach you choose to enacting strategy is likely to vary according to your circumstances.

'MANAGING ON THE EDGE'

Strategy is about positioning the organization for success. The act of positioning will entail reconciling the need for stability, which allows the company to deliver its products and services at an acceptable quality, time and cost, with the need for renewal and transformation.

One of the most thoughtful management writers of recent times, Richard Pascale, has defined the elusive qualities that successful organizations require to achieve this reconciliation between existing performance and future growth (see Figure 10.1)

Fit

This is the quality of coherence and purposefulness which enables people in an organization to work together to achieve high performance. Fit is associated with strategies which are focused and based on developed capabilities. Organizations with good fit are extremely adept at coordinating resources and deploying them where they are most required, they often have a strong culture and dominant logic. Many of the successful German companies mentioned in Chapter 4 are strong on fit.

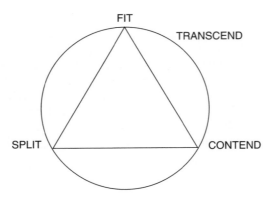

Figure 10.1 Reconciliation qualities for performance and future growth. (Based on concepts developed by Richard Pascale in *Managing on the Edge*, Penguin Books, 1991.)

Split

Split refers to the mechanisms companies create for devolving autonomy and managing diversity. Hiving off activities into separate subsidiaries, creating profit centres, forming cross-functional task forces, are examples of such devices. Split, ensures that the company is close to its markets and its customers and that decisions can be made without unwarranted delays or initiative stifled by central authority. Companies like Virgin or Hewlett Packard, for example, will regularly hive off businesses into distinct units once they have achieved a certain size.

Contend

Contend refers to the constructive tensions which are inevitable within all organizations. For example there will always be contention between the operations function (standardization, simplification, long production runs) and the marketing/sales function (differentiation, diversification, responsiveness to change). Contention should be encouraged and channelled because tension is conducive to innovation and renewal. Honda, in cars, and General Electric are both in their different ways famous for creating an atmosphere where challenging assumptions is encouraged.

Pascale's point is that successful organizations are unlikely to emphasize one of these factors to the exclusion of the others. So companies that overemphasize *fit* may be very effective at working within the existing paradigm and coordinating resources, but may be slow to perceive a change in industry logic which could leave them high and dry. Firms which stress *split*, at the expense of other features, may be flexible and responsive to customer needs; however, through a lack of coordination they may dissipate their resources: for example, activities are duplicated and different parts of the organization may work against one another and undercut each other in the market place. Moreover, because these organizations are either bound together by a strong culture or they are focused on reacting to *existing* customers, they can fail to create the conditions for renewal and growth. Organizations grounded in *contention* may be dynamic, innovative and energetic – they often create new strategies which transform industry logic – but unless they have elements of fit, this first mover advantage will be rapidly eroded by 'fast followers', prepared to invest in systems and process to dominate the new market. Similarly, unless split elements are present no one will be motivated to take the action needed to translate the idea into reality.

So to sustain success requires you to address all three elements. However to achieve success you need to do more than simply effect a balancing act. Balancing is a static, neutralizing action, reconciling the actions requires the ability to *transcend*: to address all three in the state of 'dynamic disequilibrium'. No two organizations are alike, it is likely that your success will be grounded, like the successful medium-sized firms in Chapter 4, on excelling in at least one of the dimensions – *split, fit, contend* – whilst achieving adequate performance in the other two.

So effective approaches to enacting strategy will involve:

- *Playing to the organization's strengths.* If you are effective innovators thriving on contradiction and debate you should not try to adapt an approach to implementation which would be more appropriate to McDonald's or AT&T.
- *Addressing weaknesses.* If you are successful at *fit* and *split* you don't need more planning controls and targets; rather you should look for approaches to enacting strategy which encourage innovation and diversity.
- *Building complementary alliances.* Collaborating with firms which have a different combination of *fit/split/contend* attributes or acquiring such a company is another way of enacting strategy.

Here are some guidelines for how you can enact strategy depending on the company's profile.

Bear in mind that implementing strategy will involve change for the organization and the people in it. So you are likely to find yourself at times taking measures which go with the existing culture of the business and at other times you will need to challenge that culture. For example, a 'fit' organization populated with task-orientated people will thrive on a strategy which is defined in terms of targets, deadlines and milestones. It may be the case however, that your strategy requires people to be more creative in future because in order for the firm to continue its success a new recipe will be needed. This can be uncomfortable, particularly initially.

Fit companies

Fit companies benefit from strong operational controls which enable managers to 'sweat the business'. There is often strong leadership from the top and a committed work-force. Managers know the business inside out and are hands on and 'action orientated'. In an operational sense, successful fit companies are often extremely ingenious at finding solutions to problems. Strategically the single-minded focus on a particular business and the strong culture can make the company vulnerable to a change in its environment. You cannot order a company to become more creative! But you can do things to 'destabilize' it and make the organization more open to change. You should:

■ *Encourage informal communication and spontaneous self-organization.* Increasing the channels of communication not only makes it easier to devolve authority without losing the benefits of coordination, it also multiplies the opportunities for informal communication and spontaneous self-organization: people coming together because they are motivated to find new ways of doing things, not because their department has detailed them to attend a particular committee.

■ *Avoid dictating agendas or setting specific objectives.* Rather you should identify problems or pose paradoxes for groups to resolve. For example, how can you be both a successful innovator *and* a low cost producer? Set rules and establish the constraints for the debate; don't try and predict outcomes.

■ *Promote variety.* If creativity is a product of contention, you will not get much debate amongst people who share the same mindset. You should therefore rotate people regularly so they don't get stale, and so they can both disseminate their own expertise and gain insights from other parts of the business. Bring in outsiders with a different background and culture. Involve people at the periphery of the organization who have not yet been absorbed into the culture fully.

- *Avoid over reliance on an incumbent management team.* In many firms the further up the hierarchy you go the greater the attachment to the existing logic and the closer the adherence to the status quo. It follows therefore that you should:
- *Identify change agents below the top.* The much abused middle management are usually knowledgeable and are often brimming with new ideas, they are also less committed to the status quo, so you should encourage them.
- *Tolerate parallel developments.* In a world where the future is inherently unknowable and everything is to play for, sticking too close to the knitting can be disastrous. Permit experimentation, learn from failure.
- *Subvert stability.* To challenge the status quo, you need to allow enough organizational slack for the firm to develop the future recipe alongside its existing recipe.
- *Seek to reduce anxiety.* Since transformational change is threatening it is likely to induce anxiety and defensive behaviour. You need to reduce fear by offering realistic terms: for example, continued employment in return for total flexibility.

Split companies

Split type organizations have a bias for action. They are businesses where you see things happen, a product line or service flourishes and as it achieves critical mass it is spun off to be grown and managed as a separate entity. Individual initiative is frequently encouraged and rewarded as people are given opportunities, and when they succeed, greater responsibilities. The problems that go with this kind of organization are that leadership may be unclear, there may be so many different units and activities undertaken at any one time that the nominal leader may not be fully aware of all activities. There is a danger that each unit develops into a 'feudal barony', each a law unto itself. The challenge is to encourage initiative and enable projects to grow unhindered, while achieving coherence and consistency across the business. Factors that will be important in split businesses are;

- *Communications*. These need to be open, not just up and down but across the organization, diagonally through the business. Formal written communications may be useful ways of sending out information, but you cannot rely on these to be fully digested. You need to ensure that regular informal activity and communications occur.
- *Retreats*. Bring people from all parts of the organization together from time to time to discuss business issues that affect all of them. Use these times to inform and update as well as to think afresh about ideas. Don't just involve the management hierarchy but draw on a range of people up and down and across the business.
- *Cross-functional teams*. Don't try to import complex matrix management systems with multiple reporting lines. Keep things simple. Use project teams drawn from across the organization to introduce new products or processes.
- *Centres of excellence*. Devolve responsibility for policy *company wide* to the units with the greatest expertise, rather than splitting it up or retaining it at head office.
- *Leadership*. Take time to know and become familiar with people across the organization. Continuously check out your thinking against the feelings and opinions in different parts of your organization. Balance your need to give central direction with local autonomy. Aim to provide guiding principles for success in the business: communicate these and reiterate them, use them to encourage and guide actions within the business rather than as a strait jacket or set of hurdles which all proposals must overcome.
- *Organizational Learning*. Create mechanisms within the business that promote learning from experiences throughout the firm. Lessons learned in one part should be transferred rapidly to be applied in others. Be realistic and creative as to how this might be achieved. Written memos, writing up best practice in particular areas are unlikely to communicate the message effectively in a split business. Use briefings, retreats and other times when people come together to share learning and transfer experiences.
- *Develop functions as repositories of wisdom*. The cross business functions – engineering, R&D, marketing, etc. – should be used as

vehicles for learning to cultivate and promote expertise across the firm.

Contend companies

Contend type organizations can be exciting places to work in, but they can also be frustrating. Ideas are constantly emerging and experiments initiated but implementation is often stymied by poor product launches and inattention to build quality. Apple, the computer firm, is a classic 'contend' type firm.

So the challenge is to find a more successful way of exploiting pathbreaking ideas by ensuring that the systems and controls are in place to deliver performance and that personal initiative and entreprenurialism are encouraged. You should not try to graft on a strategic planning system more appropriate to a multi-national oil company. Instead you should:

- *Implement strategy via projects.* Good ideas which are consistent with the company's mission and capabilities can be implemented through projects with defined delivery dates and accountabilities. You can use projects to test ideas before investing further.
- *Delegate power to project teams.* Reducing time to market and delivering to specification entails parallel processing or 'simultaneous engineering', this can only come about by ensuring that power and accountability reside with project teams and their leaders, not with the functions.
- *Design reward systems for cohesive performance.* You should ensure the rewards and incentives are geared as much to the group as to individual performance and show how by building on the ideas of others individuals can gain themselves.
- *Monitoring the performance of projects against milestones.* You should periodically review the progress of projects against interim targets. If, say, a project outcome is to launch a new product within two years, you can break down the achievement of the ultimate target into staging posts: 'final design agreed by X', 'regulatory approval by Y', 'piloting by Z'. Monitoring attainment against the targets will help you to avoid unpleasant surprises!
- *Consider outsourcing and alliances.* If efficiency and accountability are elusive concepts to the organization we should consider outsourcing production or licensing new ideas to other organizations who do have these capabilities.

■ *Monitor the performance of the business as a whole against a few key measures.* These are the 'bus ticket' controls referred to in Chapter 4. You need to define what business measures are critical to success. Cash flow and liquidity are always likely to be important, for example. Market share may be critical in volume industries. By benchmarking with competitors and or past performance you can measure performance and respond to problems before they become critical.

EXERCISES

Exercise 1

What kind of organization are you? You may have a fairly good idea where you stand in the 'Fit/Split/Contend' model. The following statements are strongly associated with the different types as indicated. Ask yourselves which ones apply to your organization.

1   Our organization has a clear sense of purpose. (Fit)
2   We prefer to delegate autonomy in our firm. (Split)
3   We have a very strong culture. (Fit)
4   Our organization thrives on conflict. (Contend)
5   When you meet one of our employees you know immediately they are company people. (Fit)
6   Sometimes the right arm does not know what the left arm is doing in our firm. (Split)
7   We are a 'pretty motley crew' in our firm but that is the way we like it. (Contend)
8   Top management in this firm are real control freaks. (Fit)
9   Time is critical to our business, getting to the market before our competitors is the difference between success and failure. (Split)
10   This firm is full of people with bright ideas but we don't have the completors to implement. (Contend)
11   Our strategy is based on maximizing our capabilities. (Fit)
12   By staying close to the market we can sustain our company's success. (Split)
13   A strong culture is the glue which keeps the disparate parts of this organization together. (Split)
14   We work best when we are excited by a new idea. (Contend)
15   We work best when we have clear targets to hit. (Fit)

16   We work best when the centre lets us get on with our own thing. (Split)
17   We know more or less where the company is going over the next three years. (Fit)
18   We know where our divisions are going to be in twelve months time, but beyond that anything could happen. (Split)
19   The future is unknowable. (Contend)
20   If you design a better mousetrap people will beat a path to your door. (Contend)
21   A strong culture discourages new ideas and innovations. (Contend)

Appendix A
Sources of Industry Data

- ALTA VISTA – sophisticated Internet search tool.
  http://altavista.
  digital.com
- AMADEUS – A Pan-European database of the top 150,000 public and private companies in Europe, available from Bureau Van Dijk.
- ANBAR ELECTRONIC INTELLIGENCE – abstracts of management topics including, e.g. information on trade associations.
  http://www.anbar.co.uk\anbar.htm
- DUN AND BRADSTREET – Databases of UK, European, Global and Japanese Businesses via CD-ROM or Internet. Also company reports. Dun and Bradstreet, Holmers Farm Way, High Wycombe, Bucks, HP12 4UL. Tel: + 44 (0) 1494 423681, Fax: + 44 (0) 1494 422260. World Wide Web: http://www.dbisna.com
- Economic Forecasts for the UK Economy – HM Treasury, Public Enquiry Unit. Room 11012, Parliament Street, London SW1P 3AG. Tel: 0171 270 4558. A monthly summary of over 40 independent forecasters.
- Economist Intelligence Unit. Sector reports. 15 Regents Street, London, SW1Y 4LR. Tel: + 44 (0) 171 8301000, Fax: + 44 (0) 171 4999767
- FAME (Financial Analysis Made Easy) – A financial database of major public and private British companies. Available from Bureau Van Dijk, 1 Great Scotland Yard, London, SW1A 2HN. Tel + 44 (0) 171 839 2266. Fax: + 44 (0) 171 839 6632.
- FT Profile – Online information including press in UK and Europe

and market intelligence.

- Key Note Reports on market sectors. Also available on CD-ROM. Key Note Market Information, Field House, 72 Oldfield Road, Hampton, Middlesex, TW12 2HQ. Tel. + 44 (0)181 783 0755. Fax: + 44 (0) 181 783 0049.

- MAID – Online information service which allows you to access the portion of a report you require. MAID, The Communications Building, 48 Leicester Square, London, WC2H 7DB. Tel:+ 44 (0) 171 930 6900, Fax: + 44 (0) 171 930 6006. World Wide Web: http://www.maid-plc.com.

- MAPS – Market reports on over 1000 UK sectors available on CD-ROM

- MINTEL – Reports on industry sectors, also available online and with Lotus Notes. Updated daily. Mintel International Group, 18-19 Long Lane, London, EC1A 9HE. Tel: + 44 (0) 171 606 4533, Fax: + 44 (0) 171 606 5932

- ONLINE/CD-ROM BUSINESS INFORMATION – Monthly publication reviewing key information sources, Headland Business Information, Maypole House, Maypole Road, East Grinstead, West Sussex, RH19 1HU. Tel: + 44 (0) 1342 330100, Fax: + 44 (0) 1342 330191

- UK Markets – Taylor Nelson AGB Publications, 14/17 St John's Square, London EC1M 4HE. Tel: 0171 608 0072 Fax: 0171 490 1550. Detailed market data available as hard-copy, on CD Rom and on 24-hour automated fax service providing response within 3 minutes.

References

Bracker, J. S., Keates, B. W. and Pearson, I. N. (1988) 'Planning and financial performance amongst small firms in a growth industry', *Strategic Management Journal*, Vol 9, pp. 591–603.

Carter, N. M. *et al.* (1994) 'New venture strategies theory developments with an empirical base', *Strategic Management Journal*, Vol 15, pp. 21–41.

Covin, J. G. (1991) 'Entreprenurial versus conservative firms, a comparison of strategies and performance', *Journal of Management Studies*, Vol 28, No. 5 (September), pp. 439–62.

Covin, J. G. and Slevin, D.P. (1989) 'Strategic management in small firms in hostile and benign environments', *Strategic Management Journal*, Vol 10, pp. 75–87.

Covin, J. G. and Slevin, D. P. (1990) 'Content and performance of growth seeking strategies: a comparison of small firms in high and low technology industries', *Journal of Business Venturing*, Vol 5, pp. 391–412.

Emin, C. D. (1990) 'A database of high growth independent, mid-sized UK companies', in Taylor, B. and Herbert, P., *International Strategies of Growing Companies*, Henley Management College.

Feigenbaum, A. and Karnaney, A. (1991) 'Output flexibility a competitive advantage for small firms', *Strategic Management Journal*, Vol 12, pp. 101–14.

Harrison, J. and Taylor, B. *Super Growth Companies*, Butterworth Heinemann, pp. 3–17.

Hay, M. and Kamshad, K. (1994) 'Small firm growth intentions, implementation, and impediments', *Business Strategy Review* (autumn), Vol 5, No 3, pp. 49–68.

Hogg, J. (1993) Strategy and performance in small IT firms. MBA dissertation, Henley Management College.

Hughes, L. (1990) 'A preliminary investigation into the international strategies of growing companies', in Herbert, P. and Taylor, B., *International Strategies of Growing Companies*.

Kets de Fries, M. (1996) *Family Business: Human Dilemmas in the Family Firm*, International Thomson Publishing.

McKinsey *et al.* (1993) *Einfach überlegen*, Schaffer-Poeschel Verlag, Stuttgart.

Pearce, J. A., Freeman, E. B., Robinson, R. B. (1987) 'The tenuous link between formal planning and financial performance', *The Academy of Management Review*, Vol 12, No 4, pp. 658–675, 1987.

Powell, C. P. (1992) 'Research notes and communications, strategic planning as competitive advantage', *Strategic Management Journal*, Vol 13, pp. 551–58.

Schwenk, C. R. and Shrader, C. B. (1993) 'The effects of formal strategic planning on financial performance in small firms; a meta analysis of entrepreneurship theory in practice', *Entrepreneurship: Theory and Practice*, (spring) Vol 17, No 3, pp. 53–64.

Taylor, B. *et al.* (1990) 'Strategy and leadership in growth companies', *Long Range Planning*, Vol 23, No 3, pp. 66–75.

Taylor, B., Galinsky, A. and Hilmi, A. (1987) *Strategy and leadership in growth companies*, Anglo-German Foundation, London.

Todd, A. and Taylor, B. (1993) 'The baby sharks: strategies of British Super Growth Companies', *Long Range Planning*, Vol 26, (April), pp. 69–77.

Further Reading

ON COMPETITIVE ADVANTAGE

Grant, R. M. (1995) *Contemporary Strategy Analysis*, Blackwells.
Kay, J. (1993) *The Foundations of Corporate Success*, OUP.
Porter, M. E. (1980) *Competitive Strategy*, The Free Press.

ON STRATEGIES FOR INDUSTRY STAGES

Harrigan, K. (1980) *Strategies for Declining Businesses*, Lexington Books, Lexington Mass.
Stopford, J. and Baden-Fuller, C. (1992) *Rejuvenating the Mature Business*, Routledge.
Porter, M. E. (1985) *Competitive Advantage*, Free Press.
Calori, R. (1986) 'Effective Strategies in Emerging Industries', *Long Range Planning*, Vol 19, No 6.

Index

acquisitions 45–6, 100–1, 107
analogous thinking 103–4
Ansoff, I. 56, 91
Ansoff matrix 113–14

barriers to entry 74
Boston Consulting Group (BCG) 32
Bracker, J.S. *et al.* 40
business environment
    analysing
        business cycle 55, 59–61
        PEST 61–6
        practical exercise 66–7
        uncertainty 54–9
        understanding 53–67
buyers *see* suppliers/buyers

capabilities 17–18
    durability 18
    immobility 18–19
    inimitability 19
    rarity 18
    substitutability 19–20
    valuable 19
Carter, N.M. *et al.* 43
changeability 55
competitive advantage
    attaining competitive edge 22–3
    practical exercises 23–5
    search for 15–25

strategy as fit 15–16
    from resources to capabilities 17
    identifying strengths 16–17
    as sustainable 17–20, 92–100
    using company's weaknesses 21–2
competitor analysis 76–7
    practical exercises 77–80
contend companies 118–19, 123
    consider outsourcing and alliances
        123
    delegate power to project teams 123
    design reward systems for cohesive
        performance 123
    implement strategy via projects 123
    monitor performance of business as a
        whole agains key measures 124
    monitor performance of projects
        agains milestones 123
core competencies 76
corporate success
    architecture 20
    innovation 20
    key factors 26–7
        dominant logic 27
        economies of scale/experience
            curve 30–5
        life cycle 28–30
        practical exercises 35–7
    in medium–sized companies 38–46
    reputation 20

strategic assets 20–1
cost leadership 41–3, 92, 93–7, 105–6
Covin, J.G. 43
  and Slevin, D.P. 41, 42, 44
creativity 102–5
  practical exercise 115

demographics 55
differentiation 41–3, 92, 93–7
diversification 97–100
dominant logic 27

economies of scale 30–1, 59
economy
  forecasting 47–8
    inaccessiblity 51
    practical exercise 51–2
    in practice 50
    reliability 48–9
    uncertainty and shocks 49–50
    understanding 47–52
Emin, C.D. 39
environmental uncertainty
  analysing 54–6
  managing 56–9
experience curve 31–5

Feigenbaum, A. and Karnaney, A. 42
finance 45
first mover advantage 33–4
fit companies 117, 120
  avoid dictating agendas/setting
    specific objectives 120
  avoid over reliance on incumbent
    management team 121
  identify change agents below the top
    121
  informal communication/spontaneous
    self–organization 120
  promote variety 120–1
  seek to reduce anxiety 121
  subvert stability 121
  tolerate parallel developments 121
Five Forces model 72–5
  practical exercise 77–8
  using 75
flexibility 44, 57, 59

generic strategies 90, 92–100

Harrison, J. and Taylor, B. 42
Hay, M. and Kamshad, K. 39
Hogg, J. 41
Hughes, L. 46

IBM 26–7
incrementalism 56, 58
industry
  competitive dynamics 68
    attractiveness 72–5
    competitor analysis 75–7
    market structures 68–72
    practical exercises 77–80
  growth phases 10
  life cycle 28–30
information 61
  brainstorming 61–2
  impact/importance of 62, 64
integration 99

Japanese model 34–5, 100
Johnson, G. and Scholes, K. 91
joint ventures 101–2
Just–in–Time 17

Kay, John 20
Kets de Fries, M. 45

lean production 94

McKinsey, 40
  et al. 42, 44
make or buy decisions 99
managing on the edge 117
  contend 118–19, 123–4
  fit 117, 120–1
  split 118, 121–3
market
  development 97
  share 34
  structures
    monopolistic 68–9, 70, 71
    oligopolistic 58–9, 71–2
    perfect competition 69
medium–sized companies

competition in variety of different
  industry sectors 43
defined 38–9
differentiation or cost leadership
  competition 41–3, 95
focus and consistency 40–1
focus and flexibility 44
overcoming obstacles to success 44–6
as purposeful and aggressive 43
use of strategic planning 39–40
minimum efficient scale (MES) 30–1
missions
  purpose 11
  statement 11
  values 11
  vision/direction 11
Mittelstand 35, 40
Model T Ford 33
monopolies 68–71

niche markets 70

objectives 11–13
oligopolies 58–9, 71–2
organic development 100

Pearce, J.A. *et al.* 39
perfect competition 69
PEST analysis 61–6
  practical exercise 79
planning 4–5
  long range 56, 57
  see also strategic planning
Porter, M. 72–3, 91, 92, 94
Porter's matrix 112–13
Powell, C.P. 40
predictability 55–6
product life cycle 55, 71, 97
Profit Impact of Market Strategy
  (PIMS) 34
profitability 34

resources 17

Schwenk, C.R. and Shrader, C.B. 40
split companies 118, 121–2
  centres of excellence 122

communications 122
cross–functional teams 122
develop functions as repositories of
  wisdom 122–3
leadership 122
organizational learning 122
retreats 122
Stanford Research Institute 34
strategic
  group analysis 77
  management 56–7, 58–9
  planning 39–40
    need for 5–6
    see also planning
strategy 4–5
  alternative directions 90–100, 106–7
  alternative methods 91, 100–2
  creation of new 102–5
  decision–making 13
  enacting 116–17
    managing on the edge 117–24
    practical exercise 124–5
  evaluating options
    acceptability 107–9
    example 109–12
    feasibility 109
    practical exercise 115
    suitability 105–7
  as fit 15–21
  for medium–sized companies 38–46
  MOST hierarchy 10–14
  plotting approaches to
    capital intensity 9
    competitive dynamics 10
    environmental uncertainty 8
    industry culture 9
    national cultures 10
    ownership 8
    practical exercises 8–10, 13–14, 81–8,
      112–15
    retreat 81
  styles and approaches
    formal 7
    planning horizon 7–8
    top down 6–7
  tactics 13–14
  use of scenarios 60–1
success *see* corporate success

suppliers/buyers 17
  bargaining power 74–5

Taylor, B. *et al.* 39, 40, 41, 42, 44
Todd, A. and Taylor, B. 44, 45

turbulence scale 55–6

uncertainty
  economic 49–50
  environmental 54–9